THE MUSIC OF JOONAS KOKKONEN

To Colleen and Joren

The Music of Joonas Kokkonen

EDWARD JURKOWSKI
University of Lethbridge, Canada

Routledge
Taylor & Francis Group

LONDON AND NEW YORK

First published 2004 by Ashgate Publishing

Reissued 2018 by Routledge
2 Park Square, Milton Park, Abingdon, Oxon OX14 4RN
711 Third Avenue, New York, NY 10017, USA

Routledge is an imprint of the Taylor & Francis Group, an informa business

First issued in paperback 2018

A Library of Congress record exists under LC control number: 2003063851

Notice:
Product or corporate names may be trademarks or registered trademarks, and are used only for identification and explanation without intent to infringe.

Publisher's Note
The publisher has gone to great lengths to ensure the quality of this reprint but points out that some imperfections in the original copies may be apparent.

Disclaimer
The publisher has made every effort to trace copyright holders and welcomes correspondence from those they have been unable to contact.

ISBN 13: 978-0-815-39801-1 (hbk)
ISBN 13: 978-1-138-62111-4 (pbk)
ISBN 13: 978-1-351-14596-1 (ebk)

Contents

Preface

As we look back upon the twentieth century from the vantage of a new millennium, Joonas Kokkonen's stature as one of the most significant post-1945 Finnish composers has become ever more apparent. Kokkonen is mainly known outside of Finland for his 1975 opera *Viimeiset kiusaukset* (*The Last Temptations*), by far the most successful Finnish opera, and his cycle of four symphonies, the most vital series of essays by any Finnish symphonist—save, of course, Sibelius. However, the impressive list of orchestral, chamber orchestra, and chamber works prove that beautiful and masterfully crafted compositions may be found in virtually every genre of Kokkonen's oeuvre. Oddly, however, piano music represents a small and minor position in Kokkonen's post-1957 works—a surprising fact, given the extensive number of pieces written for the instrument and Kokkonen's distinguished reputation as a piano soloist during his early career.

From 1950 to 1963 Kokkonen held various academic positions at the Sibelius Academy: he not only taught music theory and history, but was also a distinguished composition professor, who during his tenure at the Academy taught some of the most celebrated present-day Finnish composers. Through the 1950s Kokkonen was also an important and influential music critic who wrote for the two major Finnish newspapers of the day, *Ilta Sanomat* (*The Evening News*) and *Uusi Suomi* (*New Finland*). In addition, he was a noted essayist whose writings on a variety of subjects ranging from the importance of Bach in music education to philosophical issues surrounding contemporary music activities demonstrated a penetrating insight that still has relevance today.

Kokkonen's significance in Finland's musical life, however, extended far beyond his academic posts or distinguished career as a composer. For instance, in the nearly three decades that followed his appointment to the Finnish Academy in 1963, Kokkonen was tireless in his work surrounding legislative issues of copyright protection. In addition, he played a vital role in the development of an extensive music education system—in fact, a strong case can be made that the healthy and enviable status of music education currently in Finland is directly the result of Kokkonen's unceasing dedication to this aspect of his position within the Finnish Academy.

Kokkonen has, at times, been pejoratively labeled a conservative composer, an unfair point of view that the chapters which follow will hopefully repudiate. Specifically, Kokkonen has been criticized for nurturing an old-fashioned narrative conception of musical structure and expression—narrative, in this sense, assumes that significance, formal or expressive, arises out of a linked series of unfolding events—at a time when other compositional aesthetics had captured the attention of composers. However, as we generate a new historiography of twentieth-century music (and, specifically, one not focused solely on musical activities west of the Rhine) Kokkonen, like so many other twentieth-century composers, has come to be viewed in a much different and more positive perspective. In particular, Kokkonen is now seen as a composer from a country rich in twentieth-century orchestral composition who fully and knowingly entered the arena of symphonic composition during the 1950s, i.e., at a time when the European avant-garde had dismissed the genre as a musical museum piece, and yet created what has come to be viewed as the most valuable series of symphonies by a Finnish composer from the second half of the twentieth century. However, not only have Kokkonen's symphonies and orchestral compositions proven to be worthy successors to Sibelius' towering works, but as the analyses of countless works from his oeuvre demonstrate—and in my opinion, this is one of his most distinctive contributions (and yet, up to now, has been completely ignored by scholars)—Kokkonen also created an interesting and refreshing approach to dodecaphonic composition and, as a corollary, to the pitch organization of a work. In sum, Kokkonen's challenging works not only occupy a vital place in Finland's remarkable lineage of twentieth-century composition, but have also had a profound influence upon his own, as well as succeeding generations of Finnish composers.

Readers interested in a detailed biography of Kokkonen's life and his influence upon Finnish music can do no better than Pekka Hako's excellent *Voiko Varjo olla Kirkas;*[1] unfortunately, the book is in Finnish, delimiting its potential readership. And while Kokkonen is far from an unknown composer outside of Finland, his music is still not as familiar as it should be; however, Hako's biography contains no formal analyses, thus restricting the book's use even further for someone interested in Kokkonen's harmonic, rhythmic and formal designs—in other words, the sound world of Kokkonen's compositions.

The Music of Joonas Kokkonen attempts to rectify this significant lacuna in Kokkonen scholarship. The book opens with a brief chronology of twentieth-century Finnish music to provide the reader with a general background to the musical landscape during the 1950s, i.e., the time during which Kokkonen established his early reputation as a composer. Chapter two contains a biographical sketch of Kokkonen; chapter three is a survey of the salient features of his individual approaches to form and dodecaphonic composition. The next six chapters of the book contain analyses of all of Kokkonen's significant works; the chapters are organized according to genre. The final chapter contains some thoughts on Kokkonen's legacy to Finnish cultural life.

While the initial chapters (and especially chapter three) contain important expository material, the remainder of *The Music of Joonas Kokkonen* does not have to be read in a linear fashion, as the discussion of each piece is essentially self-contained. The prose is descriptive in nature and at a level for one with knowledge of rudimentary concepts of contemporary analytical writing. However, some terms have been created to address features specific to Kokkonen's music; such terms are defined in the Definitions section following the Acknowledgements.

Note

1.   Pekka Hako, *Voiko Varjo olla Kirkas: Joonas Kokkosen elämä* (Helsinki: Ajatus Kirjat, 2001).

Acknowledgements

First and foremost, I would like to acknowledge my Finnish colleague Hannu Apajalahti. It was during my early years as a Ph.D. student that Hannu, a visiting scholar from the Sibelius Academy, suggested that I listen to *The Last Temptations* as an introduction to Kokkonen's music; it was advice for which I will be forever indebted. I went down to the local classical record store, came home and was immediately transfixed by the sheer energy and power of the libretto, music and Kokkonen's simply masterful control of the orchestra. Embracing Kokkonen's music led naturally to many other twentieth-century Finnish composers ranging from Leevi Madetoja to Magnus Lindberg, as well as a passion for Finnish culture in general. Happily, following several years of studying Kokkonen's music in exhaustive detail, articles, conference papers and ultimately this book, as well as innumerable discussions with colleagues on both sides of the Atlantic Ocean, I recently listened to the opera with some friends and remained deeply moved by the experience.

Grateful thanks are due to Warner/Chappell Music Finland Oy and G. Schirmer Music, Inc., the copyright holders of Kokkonen's music, for granting me permission to reprint the numerous musical excerpts in the book. I would like to gratefully acknowledge the University of Lethbridge, which awarded me two research grants in 1998 and 2000 that allowed me to travel to Helsinki to procure the majority of the research materials for this project. To the invaluable help from the Finnish Music Information Centre and in particular, Pekka Hako and Anni Heino, I owe a debt greater than I will ever be able to repay. The library staff at the Sibelius Academy library was helpful in providing me unrestricted access to Kokkonen's extant manuscripts. Two of Kokkonen's children, Arja and Jarmo, were generous with their time and candid with their recollections about their father, providing me with a perspective that has shaped this book to a certain degree. Last, I would like to thank my wife Colleen Bakker and son Joren, for helping keep this project in perspective. It is to Colleen and Joren I dedicate this book with affection and appreciation.

Definitions

Interval Cycle
A series of pitches separated by an identical interval that returns to the original pitch; the interval number represents semitones. Some examples include: a chromatic scale is an interval-1 cycle; a whole-tone collection, for instance, C,D,E,F♯,G♯,A♮,(C), is an interval-2 cycle; a fully diminished seventh chord, for instance, C,E♭,F♯,A,(C), is an interval-3 cycle; and a series of perfect fourths, C,F,B♭,E♭,A♭,D♭,G♭,B,E,A,D,G,(C), is an interval-5 cycle.

Octatonic Collection
The octatonic collection, a favorite of composers such as Bartók and Stravinsky (to name but two), is employed in a number of Kokkonen's works. The collection is a symmetrical ordering of eight pitches; its intervals alternate between a minor second and Major second. There are three possible transpositions of the octatonic collection: C,C♯,D♯,E,F♯,G,A,B♭, labeled as $OCT_{0,1}$; C♯,D,E,F,G,G♯,B♭,B, labeled as $OCT_{1,2}$; and D,E♭,F,F♯,G♯,A,B,C, labeled as $OCT_{2,3}$.

Permutation
A common feature of Kokkonen's dodecaphonic writing is to rotate or permute a row, thereby altering its series of order positions. For instance, by rotating the pitches of the row F,E,C,A,G,D,A♭,D♭,E♭,G♭,B♭,B to C,A,G,D,A♭,D♭,E♭,G♭,B♭,B,F,E, order positions 1 and 2 would become order positions 10 and 11, respectively, order position 3 becomes order position 1, order position 4 becomes order position 2, etc. One important rationale for permuting a row is to highlight specific harmonic features and associate them with particular order positions from other row orderings or row forms.

Row Form
Any row ordering (see the entry for **Row Ordering**) contains forty-eight possible row forms: the twelve transpositions of a (P)rime row form, the twelve transpositions of an (I)nversion row form, the twelve transpositions of a retrograde version of a prime row form (RP), and the twelve transpositions of a retrograde version of an inversion row form (RI).

Row Labels

Many of Kokkonen's works utilize multiple row orderings (see the entry for **Row Ordering**) within the same movement. The system of nomenclature to identify these different rows uses a Roman numeral to designate the movement, followed by a letter for the particular row. For instance, row I/A would be the first designated row in movement one, while III/B would be the second designated row in movement three. In general, a row with an "A" designation has greater structural importance than a row with a "B" designation.

P_n

The "prime" form of the row whose first pitch begins with "n," where n ranges in value from 0 for C, 1, for C♯/D♭, 2 for D, ..., 10 for A♯/B♭, and 11 for B. For instance, if the primary tone row is G♯,A,F♯,G,B,B♭,D♭,C,E,F,D,E♭, it would be labeled P_8. Note that this row played backwards, i.e., E♭,D,F,E,C,D♭,B♭,B,G,F♯,A,G♯, is referred to as a retrograde row form of P_8 and formally labeled as RP_8.

I_n

The "inverted" form of a row whose first pitch begins with "n," where n ranges in value from 0 for C, 1, for C♯/D♭, 2 for D, ..., 10 for A♯/B♭, and 11 for B. For instance, if the primary tone row G♯,A,F♯,G,B,B♭,D♭,C,E,F,D,E♭ is inverted to also begin on G♯, the row would be G♯,G,B♭,A,F,F♯,D♯,E,C,B,D,C♯. Note that this row played backwards, i.e., C♯,D,B,C,E,D♯,F♯,F,A,B♭,G,G♯, is referred to as a retrograde row form of I_8 and formally labeled as RI_8.

Row Ordering

A series of pitch classes which generates a particular succession of interval classes. While twelve-element rows are the most common in Kokkonen's music, the length can vary from as little as six elements to as many as fourteen.

Chapter 1

Historical Background

Although art music has been a part of Finnish culture for several centuries, Jean Sibelius is widely considered the first Finnish composer of international prominence and remains the country's most celebrated composer—arguably the most famous composer from any of the Nordic countries. Sibelius' extraordinary success in the genres of the symphony and symphonic poem are important contributions to large-scale orchestral music and have become a highly valued aspect of twentieth-century Finnish culture.[1] Finnish composers know well the impact of Sibelius upon twentieth-century Finnish music—indeed, Sibelius' compositions are widely considered to be the *sine qua non* exemplar of late-romantic Finnish nationalism and as such they have also been the yardstick that has measured the output of his contemporaries and successors.[2]

Despite the achievements of Sibelius, one can identify composers even from Sibelius' generation whose music, while strongly rooted in a late-Romantic style, occasionally contained musical attributes that anticipated stylistic features found in Finnish modernist compositions from the late 1910s; two examples include Selim Palmgren's *Kuvia Suomesta* and Toivo Kuula's *Eteläpohjalainen Sarja No. 2* (both works date from 1908). In an attempt to move beyond their inherited musical tradition, such works by these (as well as other) composers display elements of harmony, orchestration and texture found in the music of Claude Debussy. And even though the first Finnish premiere of an orchestral work by Debussy took place as late as 1922 (the composition was *La Mer*), the stylistic attributes of his music that began to appear in Finnish compositions from the early 1900s are an indication of the awareness of contemporary musical activities from France long before the music would have been heard in Finland's concert halls—not an insignificant point, given that late nineteenth-century German- and Russian-styled music would account for virtually all non-Nordic music to which a Finnish composer from the early part of the twentieth century would have been exposed.[3]

With the end of World War I and Finland's independence in 1917, the country went through a number of seismic political and social changes. Not surprisingly, these substantial transformations to Finland's society were mirrored by the visual art, drama, literature and music from the time period. While many composers played a role during the 1920s and 1930s in changing the prevailing style of Finnish music, one which, as noted above, was strongly entrenched in late romanticism, Uuno Klami (1900–1961), Aarre Merikanto (1893–1958), Ernest Pingoud (1887–1942) and Väinö Raitio (1891–1945) represent a group of Finnish composers whose music has been recognized as the most significant attempt during this time period to overcome what many Finnish scholars have referred to as "The Shadow of Sibelius." These four composers founded no school and wrote music that is, perhaps not surprisingly, stylistically divergent. However, their association may be made by their attraction to the more progressive music of Debussy and Scriabin as the basis for their radical musical compositions, rather than such late nineteenth-century composers as Reger, Strauss and Tchaikovsky, the foreign composers who would have been favored by most Finnish composers from this time, as well as Sibelius. In short, while nationalism was still held as paramount, there was a general mood for change in the air, where a new generation of composers was ready to embrace novel influences outside of Finland.

While the popularity of Sibelius' musical style, both within Finland and abroad, may have elevated the composer's status to near mythical proportions, Erkki Salmenhaara has noted that, paradoxically, Sibelius' influence on younger Finnish composers such as the above-mentioned four modernists was marginal.[4] For instance, composers such as Merikanto, Pingoud and Raitio all openly acknowledged Sibelius' use of overt tonal structures as, for instance, in the fifth symphony, was a major disappointment and could not (or refused to) see the significance of the composer's later output.[5] Einar Englund has described a personal accounting of their reaction to Sibelius' later music as follows:

> After the first performance of the fourth symphony by Sibelius Väinö Ratio and Aarre Merikanto were sitting in a restaurant and celebrating the occasion with a glass of wine. Both radicals were of the opinion that Sibelius with his new symphony had proved that their belief in the validity of music which shunned tonality was right. "If he goes on along this line, the fifth will have already moved towards atonality," they thought, and waited excitedly for the next work. The fifth came, and with it disappointment. The fourth symphony thus was a sheer experiment, a brain wave of their idol. Disappointed, they turned their gaze in the direction of Schoenberg and Hindemith—and, specifically, the latter's early expressionistic compositions—and continued persistently to write their bold works.[6]

To claim that these modernists had difficulty getting their music accepted is no mere understatement. Simply stated, Finnish composers during the 1920s and 1930s had to contend with an audience that placed Sibelius' music—and specifically, his overtly tonal compositions—on the highest order, a demand that was exacerbated by a country proud of the independence it had attained in 1917. As Glenn Koponen has noted, following the country's independence in 1917:

> [N]ational unity and cooperation in all areas of Finnish society were essential factors in light of the Russian and German oriented tensions which were continually pervasive during the first half of the century. Thus the official façade of musical life remained one of national romanticism during the period between the two world wars.[7]

With their edict for dramatic changes to the stylistic norms of Finnish composition, it would seem inevitable that these young composers would be controversial and harshly received by both audiences and critics. In fact, several of their works remained unperformed until the last few decades. An often-cited example of such neglect is Merikanto's acknowledged masterpiece, his 1922 opera *Juha*, a work which received its first complete staged production as late as 1962, and four years after the composer's death. Although not immune to the negative criticism many modernists encountered, Klami's music enjoyed more success in the concert hall than his contemporaries. For instance, Klami's most famous piece, the *Kalevala Suite* Op. 35, has been actively performed both within Finland and abroad (the work was even programmed several times in the United States by Leopold Stokowski during the 1940s). It should be noted, however, that for as much as he had embraced progressive compositional features of Ravel and Stravinsky, Klami also used themes from Finland's national folk epic *The Kalevala* in his music to a far greater degree than most other modernist composers—and especially when compared with Merikanto, the Russian-born Pingoud (who may be the sole composer from this time who never once used elements of Finland's famous folk epic in his music), and Raitio—which may have provided a more familiar basis for audiences anticipating such musical attributes and thus engendering a more favorable response to his work, at least within Finland.

While the fifteen years from 1915 to 1930 represented an unprecedented period of musical growth in Finland, the harsh criticism that the modernist composers faced inevitably took its toll: by around 1930 one can detect a pronounced change to a more reactionary style in their music.[8] Consider, for instance, the differences between Merikanto's *Abduction of Kyllikki*, an orchestral work written in 1935 to commemorate the one hundredth anniversary of the *Kalevala*: as Salmenhaara has observed, the composition is much less adventuresome, as regards harmony and rhythm, when compared with a work such as Merikanto's tone poem *Pan* from fifteen years earlier.[9]

The paucity of experimental works by composers such as Merikanto and Raitio came to nearly a complete cessation by the end of the 1930s, prompting the Finnish composer Sulho Ranta (1901–1960) to write:

> To put it in general terms: the work "modern" has lately vanished entirely from the annals concerning our young composers. I cannot, however, have another opinion of a young tone-smith's first concert of his works, where one sits "with a sage mind," than that it somehow tastes strange. One has time later on to cool down 'intellectually speaking.' And recalling other branches of our art, so far there is not yet as much of romanticism as among the youngest of our music: the poets still go on with their free metres and among the painters there are even surrealists![10]

In addition to the hostile reception many modernist composers received during the 1940s, they also faced a more practical problem: like continental Europe, there was a drastic decrease of musical activity in Finland during World War II—a situation greatly exacerbated by its complex political role between Germany and Russia—as many musicians were called to active service duty during this seven-year time period.

The end of World War II seems to have sparked a major moment in Finnish culture. Specifically, there was a general sense that it was time to move away from nationalistic styled art that had dominated the first half of the century; music, more than the other art forms, seemed galvanized to catch up with continental Europe's lead. As Kalevi Aho writes, "New trends followed one another in Finnish music in such rapid succession that several styles were always simultaneously present, and the general image of Finnish music has been pluralistic ever since the [end of the] war."[11]

With a musical landscape ripe for change, the appearance of Einar Englund's first two symphonies, dating from 1946 and 1948, was heralded as a pivotal moment in Finnish music. An important feature of these two works—indeed, his compositional style in general—is that Englund consciously set out to free himself from the established styles of Sibelius and Leevi Madetoja (1887–1947), and did so by instead relying upon the Russians Stravinsky, Prokofiev and, especially, Shostakovich. Further, stylistic attributes by these composers are cast within formal designs, orchestration and textures that demonstrate Englund's proclivity towards European neoclassicism.

Englund is usually acknowledged as the first Finnish composer whose style was more predisposed to Shostakovich's music than his Finnish predecessors. For instance, the melodic and rhythmic ideas from the two symphonies demonstrate that he knew his Shostakovich well (the first and ninth symphonies are particularly relevant here); Englund also wrote an unpublished study of the composer as early as 1946.

During the 1940s and 1950s Englund's neoclassical-styled compositions were of great interest for many younger Finnish composers looking to Europe for musical influences; four prominent composers include Nils-Eric Foufstedt (1910–1961), Nils-Eric Ringbom (1907–1988), Ahti Sonninen (Sonninen (1914–1984) is the composer of arguably Finland's most performed ballet score, the 1952 *Pessi ja Illusia*) and Jouko Tolonen (1912–1986), as well the early works of Usko Meriläinen (b. 1930) and Kokkonen. However, a significant boost to the influx of new musical trends in Finland was the founding in 1949 of the Society of Contemporary Music, an organization in which Englund played a founding role. The Society not only arranged concerts, but also brought prominent foreign composers and performers into Finland who specialized in contemporary music.

One Finnish composer who also played a role in the early years of the Society was Eric Bergman (b. 1911). Bergman is usually attributed as the first Finnish composer to utilize dodecaphonic procedures extensively in his music, a compositional style he learned primarily from his studies in 1954 with Wladimir Vogel. Vogel, in fact, became an important foreign teacher for several Finnish composers during the 1950s. For instance, following Bergman, Tauno Marttinen, Einojuhani Rautavaara and Meriläinen all traveled to Switzerland for private instruction (all these composers were leading dodecaphonic Finnish composers during the second half of the 1950s and the 1960s).

Marttinen, Rautavaara and Meriläinen all began their respective careers as neoclassical composers but altered their styles during the 1950s once they recognized the variety of modes of expression that became available to them via dodecaphonic composition. However, Paavo Heininen (b. 1938) is another composer who rose to prominence during the 1950s who should be acknowledged. Even from his earliest works, Heininen has displayed a much greater proclivity towards the modernist stance of the Darmstadt serialists than his Finnish heritage. In fact, a strong argument can be made to consider Heininen as one of the first composers to have successively shunned all traces of Sibelius' influence, a tradition that had been such a vital part of Finnish composition during the first half of the twentieth century. Not only has Heininen (himself a student of Kokkonen) had a distinguished career as a composer, but he has also taught the vast majority of the internationally prominent composers who studied at the Sibelius Academy during the final thirty years of the twentieth century—a roster that includes Eero Hämeenniemi (b. 1951), Jouni Kaipainen (b. 1956), Magnus Lindberg (b. 1958), Kaija Saariaho (b. 1952), and Jukka Tiensuu (b. 1948).

Notes

1. Present day statistics bear witness to such a statement. Although Finland has a population of approximately five and half million inhabitants, it contains twelve professional orchestras (several of international stature) and an equivalent number of semi-professional orchestras, indicating that there is indeed something quite special about the state of musical affairs in this Nordic country.
2. For discussion regarding the impact of Sibelius upon Klami, see Helena Tyrväinen, "A l'ombre de Sibelius, Uuno Klami à Montmartre" *Boreales* 54–57 (1993), pp. 109–135.
3. A substantial portion of volume 24 (2000) of *Cahiers Debussy* is devoted to the reception of Debussy's works in the Nordic countries. In particular, see Helena Tyrväinen, "Les origines de la réception de Debussy en Finlande (1901–1933)" *Cahiers Debussy* 24 (2000), pp. 3–23.
4. See Erkki Salmenhaara, "Finnish Music in the 20s and 30s: Internationalism vs. Nationalism," article contained in Tomi Mäkelä, ed., *Music and Nationalism in 20th-Century Great Britain and Finland* (Hamburg: von Bockel Verlag, 1997).
5. While it is beyond the scope of this book to discuss the more advanced aspects of the later compositions by Sibelius, for instance, issues of large-scale formal structure or long-range time spans, it should be acknowledged that these features have been either ignored or placed on a lower level of importance when compared with more surface aspects of his music—for instance, triadic harmonies or nationalistic folk influences, features which critics, for decades, have used as exemplars of a reactionary style of composition, and which have been viewed in a much different light only within the last fifteen years or so. Some examples of the literature that discuss the more progressive features of Sibelius' music include: James Hepokoski, *Sibelius: Symphony No. 5* (Cambridge: Cambridge University Press, 1993); Tim Howell, *Jean Sibelius: Progressive Techniques in the Symphonies and Tone Poems* (New York: Garland, 1989); Timothy L. Jackson and Veijo Murtomäki, *Sibelius Studies* (Cambridge: Cambridge University Press, 2001); and Veijo Murtomaki, *Symphonic Unity: The Development of Formal Thinking in the Symphonies of Sibelius* (Helsinki: University of Helsinki, 1993).
6. The Englund quote is cited in Salmenhaara, "Finnish Music in the 20s and 30s: Internationalism vs. Nationalism," p. 176.
7. Glenn Koponen, "A Study of the Symphony in Finland from 1945 to 1975 with an Analysis of Representative Compositions" (Ed.D. Dissertation, Columbia University Teachers College, 1980), p. 44.
8. For discussion of the political changes found in Finland at this time see: W. R. Mead, *Finland* (London: Ernest Benn Ltd., 1968), pp. 149–178; chapters six and seven from Fred Singleton, *A Short History of Finland* (Cambridge: Cambridge University Press, 1989); and Eric Solsten and Sandra Meditz, eds., *Finland: A Country Study* (Washington D.C.: Library of Congress Publication, 1990), pp. 16–41.
9. Salmenhaara, "Finnish Music in the 20s and 30s: Internationalism vs. Nationalism," p. 181.

10. Sulho Ranta, "Syyskauden alku," *Suomalainen Suomi* 7 (1939), cited in Salmenhaara, "Finnish Music in the 20s and 30s: Internationalism vs. Nationalism," p. 182.
11. Kalevi Aho, "Finnish Music in the Postwar Years," contained in Kalevi Aho, Pekka Jalkanen, Erkki Salmenhaara and Keijo Virtamo, *Finnish Music* (Helsinki: Otava, 1996), p. 78.

Chapter 2

Biographical Sketch

Joonas Kokkonen was born the youngest of five children on 13 November 1921 in Iisalmi; the city is almost equidistant between Helsinki and the Arctic Circle. Along with Kokkonen, it is also the birthplace of the renowned Finnish writer and poet Juhani Aho (1861–1921). Kokkonen's family moved to Järvenpää in 1926, a charming city approximately forty kilometers north of Helsinki (Sibelius also lived in the city from 1904 until his death in 1957). A few years after he graduated from the Järvenpää Community School, Kokkonen entered the University of Helsinki, where he studied music history, philosophy and literature. Military service during the early 1940s interrupted his academic study for a couple of years: while Kokkonen spoke little about his war experiences, the horrors he observed as a soldier profoundly shaped the pacifistic sentiments he carried throughout his life (one of Kokkonen's daughters once recounted a humorous story that his lack of aggression was so ingrained that he was even incapable of setting mouse traps for fear of harming a family of mice that had once infested their Helsinki residence). Despite the time spent serving in the war, Kokkonen ultimately received his M.A. degree in music history in 1948. While at the University of Helsinki, however, Kokkonen was simultaneously enrolled at the Sibelius Academy, where he obtained a diploma in piano performance in 1949 (he also studied composition briefly with Selim Palmgren, although Kokkonen would later state that he had learned virtually nothing from him).

Kokkonen's piano instructor was Ilmari Hannikainen (1892–1955), one of the finest Finnish pianists from the first half of the twentieth century, who was not only known in Finland, but also toured extensively throughout Europe and the United States. As well as a celebrated pianist, Hannikainen was a composer, with numerous songs and short piano pieces to his credit, as well as some short orchestral compositions. While there is no evidence to suggest that Kokkonen received any instruction or even encouragement from Hannikainen about his own compositions during his studies with the pianist, one cannot help but believe that Hannikainen's successful dual career as pianist and composer would have influenced Kokkonen as he was establishing himself as a concert soloist and chamber musician: every composition until the 1957 *Music for String Orchestra* is written either for piano solo, voice and piano, or features the piano prominently in a chamber work. In short, Kokkonen's early career was as a pianist—during the 1940s and 1950s he received much recognition for his performances of the Viennese classics, as well as Brahms and Chopin. However, as his compositions became better known during the 1950s he also became increasingly in demand as an interpreter of his own music.

Following a two-year engagement, Kokkonen and his first wife Marie (né Pananen) were married in 1944; by 1950 they had three children—two boys and one girl. In order to supplement his meager and unpredictable income as a pianist to support his young family, in 1946 Kokkonen began work as a music critic for the Finnish newspaper *Ilta Sanomat* (*The Evening News*); further similar appointments include chief critic for *Uusi Suomi* (*New Finland*) from 1957 to 1963 and chief editor for the journal *Uusi Musiikkilehti* (*New Music Periodical*) from 1954 to 1956. Additional stability came in 1950 when Kokkonen began teaching music history and theory at the Sibelius Academy, an appointment that he held until 1959.

The stresses of an erratic income combined with Kokkonen's increasing troubles with alcohol, however, reached a breaking point by the early 1950s and Marie filed for a divorce in 1953 (Kokkonen's tribulations with alcohol appear to have begun during his years of military service and plagued him throughout his life; they became increasingly problematic in the final decade of his life). Kokkonen remarried in 1954 to Maija (né Heljo) and together they had two daughters. By all accounts, Maija and Joonas led a tranquil and idyllic marriage—however it seems clear that it was Maija who shouldered the greater responsibility to bring constancy and structure to their home life. For instance, Joonas was frequently prone to indolence and Maija more than occasionally was the disciplinarian who kept him to a regular work schedule, especially when composition deadlines loomed.

From 1959 until 1963 Kokkonen served as professor of composition at the Academy. A number of important post-1960 Finnish composers studied with Kokkonen during his tenure, a roster which includes such names as Henrik Otto Donner (b. 1939), Paavo Heininen (b. 1938), Aulis Sallinen (b. 1935), Erkki Salmenhaara (1941–2002) and Leif Segerstam (b. 1944)—although it should also be noted that once he left his teaching appointment in 1963 Kokkonen continued to teach composition privately to a few students (two noted composers include Pehr Henrik Nordgren (b. 1944) and Mikko Heiniö (b. 1948)). Kokkonen placed great demands upon his students; he believed that mastery of counterpoint and form (both *Formenlehre* designs as well as the more general, abstract definition of the term), through extensive study of the music of Bach and the early Viennese composers (in particular, Mozart) was fundamental preparation for a composer. Paavo Heininen, for instance, has described how form was the primary focus of Kokkonen's teaching in general, to the extent that the subject was a fundamental topic even in a basic counterpoint course he took from Kokkonen at the Academy. Perhaps not surprisingly, Kokkonen expected that composers would have such skills mastered when they came to study with him; as such, preparatory study of this music was rarely part of private composition lessons. Instead, a significant portion of the training a student would have received concerned detailed study of motivic and harmonic development and formal design in their latest composition, and how these attributes might bear relationships with a work by, say, Bach or Mozart.

Kokkonen's watershed composition was his 1957 *Music for String Orchestra*, his first orchestral work following nearly two decades of pieces for voice and piano, piano solo, or the aforementioned three chamber works. *Music for String Orchestra* was quickly followed by such important compositions as the first two symphonies (1960 and 1961), the orchestral song cycle *The Hades of the Birds* (1959), *Sinfonia da camera* (1962) and the first string quartet (1959), and elevated Kokkonen to the forefront of Finnish composition during the early 1960s—a status that he retained for nearly three decades.

The premiere of *Music for String Orchestra* was also significant for Kokkonen on another account. While Nils-Eric Fougstedt conducted an ensemble of strings drawn from the Finnish Radio Symphony Orchestra, the concert master of the orchestra at that time was Paavo Berglund, who became the musical director of the orchestra the next year. Kokkonen and Berglund struck up a personal and professional friendship immediately: not only did Berglund premier each of Kokkonen's four symphonies and virtually every orchestral work, but the conductor was tireless in promoting and performing his music in Finland as well as numerous venues throughout Europe, thereby dramatically increasing Kokkonen's visibility.

A second important professional association was with the conductor Rudolf Baumgartner, the long-time musical director of the Lucerne Festival Strings. Kokkonen first heard the ensemble in 1960 and was immediately captivated by the high quality of the ensemble, and in particular, their performances of Bach and Bartók, two composers whom Kokkonen held in the highest esteem throughout his life. Although Baumgartner was responsible for commissioning only two of Kokkonen's works, the 1962 *Sinfonia da camera* and 1977 *...durch einen Spiegel...*, he, like Berglund, was an indefatigable proponent of Kokkonen's music, and performed his compositions in numerous concerts and contemporary music festivals throughout Europe.

Kokkonen's significance to Finland's musical life, however, extended far beyond his academic posts or celebrated career as a composer. For instance, along with his appointment to the Finnish Academy of Sciences in 1963, a position that guaranteed a comfortable lifetime pension whereby he could be freed from his teaching obligations at the Sibelius Academy, Kokkonen was appointed chairperson of a number of vital committees and boards. Through his untiring work on these committees he appreciably advanced several legislative issues surrounding composers, and specifically measures for equitable systems of copyright protection, commissioning structure and state-legislated grants. Further, Kokkonen played a significant role in overseeing the planning of Finland's extensive music education system—in fact, a strong case can be made that the healthy and enviable status of early music training in present-day Finland is largely the result of Kokkonen's unceasing dedication to this aspect of his position within the Finnish Academy. Finally, Kokkonen was the first artistic director of the Jyväskylä Summer Festival (Jyväskylä is a city in the interior of Finland approximately three hundred and fifty kilometers north of Helsinki; the festival began in 1965), an annual music festival that was vital for introducing contemporary music to a population that did not have immediate access to such musical activities. But for all his important accomplishments during Kokkonen's appointment to the Finnish Academy, along with the numerous other musical organizations for which he served, there was a down side: it took away from his time as a composer. In short, while Kokkonen's oeuvre is among the most distinguished of any post-Sibelian Finnish composer, it is not large and can be directly attributed to both the time he invested into his various administrative positions as well as his notorious self criticism.

By the early 1970s, Kokkonen was recognized as the pre-eminent living Finnish composer, whose cycle of four symphonies was heralded as the greatest body of work in the genre after Sibelius; the high status of these four works remains unchallenged: to date they are the most performed cycle of symphonies in Finland following Sibelius. However, Kokkonen's orchestral and chamber works are also among the most successful written by a Finnish composer: for instance, the cello concerto from 1969 is the most performed Finnish cello concerto, while the 1976 third string quartet is second only to Sibelius' quartet *Voces intimae* in number of performances. For all of Kokkonen's recognition as a symphonic composer, however, nothing prepared Finnish audiences for the explosive achievement of his 1975 opera *Viimeiset kiusaukset* (*The Last*

Temptations), the work widely considered to be his masterpiece. The composition elevated Kokkonen's distinguished stature in Finland to near mythic proportions: not only has the opera been performed hundreds of times in Finland, but it has also been staged abroad in the other Nordic countries, as well as in England, Switzerland and Germany and New York.

The success of Kokkonen's opera came at critical moment in Finland: during the 1970s Sallinen had also garnered international acclaim for two Finnish historical operas, the 1975 *Ratsumies* (*The Horseman*) and *Punainen viiva* (*The Red Line*) from 1978. The critical praise that these operas received, combined with the growing international praise of both the Savonlinna Opera Festival and the Finnish National Opera, set the country on a course during the 1970s that has often been referred to as Finland's "Opera Boom": for the past thirty years there has been a growing audience in Finland with a seemingly insatiable appetite for both traditional and new operas (consider, for example, that in the year 2000, there were fifteen new Finnish operas produced—an impressive number to consider by any country, but particularly staggering given the relatively small population of Finland). In his book *Finnish Opera*, Pekka Hako reflects on the success of opera as an art form in Finland during the latter portion of the twentieth century. He suggests that:

> There are at least two possible explanations for the opera boom. Firstly, the newness of Finland's opera tradition—only about a century long—allowed contemporary opera to establish itself and thrive. Audiences unshackled by tradition are unprejudiced and open to new things. Secondly, the success of Finnish operas abroad is due to their national subjects. Finland's geopolitical position between East and West has served to reinforce the identity of the Finnish nation; Eastern and Western influences have merged into a powerful national form of expression.[1]

While *The Last Temptations* represents a pivotal moment for Finnish opera in general, it also demarcates the downturn that began in Kokkonen's productivity. Specifically, while at least one orchestral work and/or symphony had appeared approximately each year since the 1957 *Music for String Orchestra*, only three such compositions were written after the opera: two chamber-orchestra works, the 1977 *...durch einen Spiegel...* and *Il paesaggio* from 1987, and the Requiem for full orchestra, chorus and soloists, written between 1979 and 1981. Kokkonen's compositional output began to decrease dramatically in the late 1970s. However, it virtually ceased altogether after his Requiem from 1981, a piece written in memory of Maija who had died from cancer in 1979. The only works of consequence that followed are the *Improvvisazione* for violin and piano, a short piece written for an international violin competition held in the United States at Indiana University in 1982, and the aforementioned *Il Paesaggio*, a commission for the inaugural ceremony that opened the Järvenpää Concert Hall. Clearly Kokkonen's numerous administrative duties played a crucial part in his waning output during these years. However, it has been suggested that Kokkonen's extremely high position in the Finnish musical community—by the late 1970s he was the most performed Finnish orchestral composer after Sibelius and, as just noted, the composer of the most successful Finnish opera of all time—also had a paralyzing effect upon the notoriously self-critical composer; with time, the increased paucity of new works led to ever greater bouts of insecurity that seemed to only receive comfort with alcohol. In some ways, Kokkonen's final years parallel that of Sibelius: the achievement of both composers reached a pinnacle as regards their respective styles (with Sibelius, the final three symphonies and the symphonic poem *Tapiola*; with Kokkonen, the third and fourth symphonies and *The Last Temptations*), after which, there is a dramatic lack of new works. Further, both composers lived their remaining lives in adulation receiving numerous awards (ironically, both also resided in Järvenpää), while being recognized as the preeminent Finnish composers of their respective time.

Kokkonen married for the third time in 1980, to Anita (né Mannelin). Although their years together were happy, during the final decade of his life he began to suffer increased medical complications from years of excessive alcohol and tobacco consumption; his final few years were particularly marred with physical ailments. After a lengthy illness, Kokkonen died on 2 October 1996.

Note

1.   Pekka Hako, *Finnish Opera*, translated by Jaakko Mäntyjärvi (Helsinki: Finnish Music Information Centre, 2002), p. 20.

Chapter 3

Stylistic Features

Apart from a brief period of study with Selim Palmgren while at the Sibelius Academy, Kokkonen was essentially self-taught as a composer. Aside from the inescapable Sibelius, his most significant influences—in other words, the composers that Kokkonen studied most extensively—were J. S. Bach, Bartók, Hindemith, Mozart and Shostakovich. Eager to come to terms with the growing wave of interest in twelve-tone composition that began to appear in Finland during the 1950s, Kokkonen also studied numerous scores by Schoenberg—in particular, his piano music.

Many commentators identify three stylistic periods in Kokkonen's oeuvre. His first period, dating until 1957, is marked by formal designs and textures reminiscent of neoclassicism, along with a harmonic and melodic language that demonstrates Kokkonen knew his Hindemith well. All of the compositions from this first period are for piano solo, voice and piano, or a chamber work that features the piano (the three chamber works include the 1948 Piano Trio, 1951/53 Piano Quintet and 1955 *Duo* for Violin and Piano). Tertian-styled triads feature prominently in all the works. However, as Kokkonen's compositional style developed, there was an increased use of the complete chromatic aggregate to structure the themes in these works—a comparison between the three above-mentioned chamber works proves illuminating in this regard—and suggests that his adoption of dodecaphonic techniques in the 1957 four-movement *Music for String Orchestra* is as much the result of his evolution as a composer as an attempt to be *au courante* with the twelve-tone bandwagon in Finland during the 1950s.

Kokkonen's second, "dodecaphonic," period is traditionally acknowledged to begin with the first string quartet of 1959 and end with the 1966 second string quartet. This portion of his oeuvre is usually described to contain (depending upon the author) his more "abstract," "academic," or "intellectual" works, largely due to the complex textures, consistently dissonant harmonic language, and long, angular melodies that typify these compositions. The third and final period is described to begin with the 1967 third symphony. The plethora of tertian-styled triads, albeit non-functional from a traditional tonal perspective, combined with a compositional approach that favors short motives with limited intervallic scope, characterize these works.

While there is some merit to a tripartite division of Kokkonen's compositions, the demarcations are also problematic, for they over-simplify both the nature of his compositions and his evolution as a composer. Consider, for instance, the numerous tertian sonorities in the works from the late 1960s and the 1970s. By stating that a stylistic shift away from dodecaphonic construction to a "freely tonal" approach began with the 1967 third symphony, and to focus attention towards these tertian sonorities, implies a decreased use of dodecaphonic procedures in these works. However, analysis clearly illuminates that this is not the case whatsoever. Rather, if anything, Kokkonen's approach to twelve-tone composition deepened considerably during the late 1960s and the 1970s. For instance, there is an even greater number of different row orderings and diversity in their lengths in several of the post-1967 compositions when compared with the "official" dodecaphonic works from 1959 to 1966 (the range is from six to fourteen pitches). Further, as will be discussed below in the section entitled "Twelve-Tone Composition," Kokkonen's use of multiple row orderings within a movement became a powerful means to generate intra- as well as inter-movement harmonic relationships. In short, by utilizing a larger number of diverse row orderings in these later works, there is a concomitant increase in their harmonic complexity that has gone virtually unnoticed.

In sum, instead of the traditional three, it is more profitable to consider that there are, in fact, only two stylistic periods in Kokkonen's career. The first period encompasses the early works until 1956—in other words, his neoclassical works (although given that dodecaphonic writing is such a significant feature of his later works, it might be appropriate to state that these early compositions are from his non-dodecaphonic period). Kokkonen's second period begins with the 1957 *Music for String Orchestra* and encompasses the remainder of his oeuvre. The choice of the four-movement string orchestra piece as the point to initiate a new stylistic period may seem unusual, given the work is typically viewed as Kokkonen's neoclassical work par excellence, as well as the work that best demonstrates Bartók's influence upon his music. However, *Music for String Orchestra* is the first work to utilize extensively dodecaphonic procedures as the means by which to structure pitch material (as illuminated in the discussion of the work, the pitch material in two of the four movements is almost entirely generated from twelve-tone rows): as such, it is more appropriate to place the work as the watershed composition to a new compositional approach distinct from his neoclassical works.

To coalesce two periods into one is not simply an exercise in academic hair splitting. Rather, it acknowledges that Kokkonen's post-1957 works are united by a variety of different dodecaphonic approaches—for instance, the nature of the different row orderings, the choice of row form(s) of each of these particular row orderings, or the relationships of the row orderings with other rows, both within a movement and between movements. However, a bipartite division of Kokkonen's oeuvre also allows us to understand how, and to what degree, tertian sonorities are utilized within the vast spectrum of dodecaphonic works. Just as there are different approaches to twelve-tone composition that Kokkonen explored during his career, there are numerous ways by which tertian sonorities are utilized in these post-1957 compositions; some examples include (note that a work may contain one or a combination of the following examples): works that contain only a few tertian sonorities; works that contain rows which are designed with tertian sonorities as the constituent elements to generate the row itself; works that use tertian sonorities as the means by which to harmonize a tone row; and, finally, works that contain tertian-based harmonic progressions which are independent of any twelve-tone construct. More extensive discussion as regards dodecaphonic procedures and tertian sonorities appears in the next section.

Stylistic Features of Kokkonen's Music

Pitch

Twelve-Tone Composition Unlike a number of his compatriots during the 1950s, Kokkonen never undertook any formal studies about twelve-tone music; rather, his education was entirely self-directed. As a result, Kokkonen's idiosyncratic style is simultaneously an adoption as well as an extension of the elements from Schoenberg's music that he had studied.

One of the fundamental precepts of dodecaphonic composition is that the forty-eight possible row forms of a twelve-tone row ordering (i.e., twelve Prime, twelve Inversion, twelve Retrograde Prime and twelve Retrograde Inversion) provide a self-contained system of intervallic and harmonic relationships that may be conceptualized as an analog to the harmonic relationships generated from a key center from tonal music. Certain problems with this model arise, however, when a twelve-tone composition contains more than one row ordering. Typically, such works are usually seen the result of extra-musical considerations—consider, for instance, the programmatic elements that motivate the various row orderings in the different movements of Berg's *Lyric Suite* or the numerous twelve-tone leitmotifs in his opera *Lulu*.

Kokkonen's twelve-tone works present a far greater test to the concept of "dodecaphonic organic unity." At first, such a challenge may not be that apparent, as only a minimal number of row forms typically represent a row ordering, an attribute that might lend the casual observer to suggest a lack of sophistication or complexity. However, what is highly unusual in these compositions is not only Kokkonen's use of different row orderings in different movements (not an uncommon occurrence for one even slightly acquainted with Berg's music), but also his penchant to employ *several different* row orderings within each individual movement. At times these divergent orderings articulate formal design; however, not infrequently, these different rows appear simultaneously, generating complex levels of harmonic dialogue.

Tertian sonorities Although all his works from 1936–1955 are tonally based, Kokkonen rarely used functional dominants to articulate a tonal center. Rather, tonality is expressed centrically—and primarily by asserting sonorities whose roots stand in neighbor-note relationships with each other. While root relationships of a fourth or fifth are occasionally used between successive harmonies in a chord progression, a significant percentage of them are related by thirds—and virtually always to generate invariant relationships between elements from successive triads.

An interesting feature of Kokkonen's works is his predilection to end a phrase, section, or movement with either an A Major or E Major triad; the latter triad is used as the final sonority in the vast majority of Kokkonen's slow movements, suggesting an extra-musical association with this particular triad. Importantly, even though there are consistent sonorities that end a phrase or harmonic progression, closure is not obtained by a functional harmonic progression but, rather, via a strategy that combines a long-range melodic baseline with sonorities that feature enharmonic pitch relationships.

Although a vital percentage of the pitch material from Kokkonen's post-1957 works is generated via twelve-tone techniques, a nagging problem for analysts has been the use of tertian sonorities in these compositions; in particular, they feature prominently in slow movements. Most often, such tertian sonorities function as harmonic support for the various rows deployed—i.e., a pitch from the triad (typically, the uppermost pitch) will double elements of a dodecaphonically-generated melody line. However, a progression of tertian sonorities may appear independent of dodecaphonic construction. Both instances, though, are

similar to the type of progression that typifies the neoclassical works—
namely a succession of harmonies whose roots are virtually all associated
by seconds and (especially) thirds.   This consistency of harmonic
progression throughout Kokkonen's career and, specifically, between
dodecaphonic and non-dodecaphonic passages does lead to speculation
whether the choice of row orderings was designed in accordance with these
harmonic progressions, or whether a harmonization of a tone row was made
secondarily.   Unfortunately, with the nearly complete absence of extant
sketches—Kokkonen's typical practice was to compose directly into full
score; virtually all sketches were destroyed—we can only speculate upon
such an alluring topic.

Folk/Programmatic Elements

Like the works by many other post-World War II Finnish composers,
Kokkonen's neoclassical and dodecaphonic compositions were to a large
degree a reaction against the widespread romantic-styled music that had
dominated Finnish art music prior to World War II. For instance, as far as I
have been able to ascertain, the singular folk quotation from his oeuvre is
the hymn tune *Paavon virsi* (*Paavo's Hymn*) used in *The Last
Temptations.*[1] The point is not insignificant, for it can explain, at least in
part, Kokkonen's almost fanatical denial of any extra-musical association
with his compositions, apart from the most superficial of relationships, as
well as the dismissive attitude he held towards those works which were
programmatic in design. Consider, for instance, the pre-concert lecture
about his third symphony that Kokkonen gave before the Scottish National
Orchestra's premiere performance of the work in 1969; the text is
representative of his modernist stance.

> I have myself sometimes compared a composition to a tree: the composition
> grows from its basic motifs like a tree from a seed. All the possibilities of a
> full-grown tree are already contained in its seed. The seed contains an
> enormous amount of power for growth; but, and I think this is even more
> extraordinary, it also sets certain limits on growth. The tree cannot carry on
> growing indefinitely. Perhaps this comparison will also serve to show how
> intimately the "inner" and "outer" aspects of the structure of the work depend
> upon each other. The motivic "seed" also sets limits on the "outer" structure.
>   When I was a young composer, many older composers and some of my
> own generation looked, with Sibelius, to Nature for inspiration. I was very
> critical of this attitude and used to say, "Why don't they learn counterpoint
> instead of wandering about in the forests?" But as one gets older, one finds
> that one's views mellow and, although I'm almost ashamed to admit it, my
> third symphony was born as the result of a particularly vivid experience of

Nature during the summer of 1965. However, I don't suppose I could put that experience into words even if I tried. In spite of its inspiration, the third symphony is absolute music. The link with Nature is most apparent in the orchestral colour, which I use much more freely than in my earlier symphonic works.

In point of fact, aside from program notes Kokkonen rarely spoke about his own music; further comments from the pre-concert lecture are typical of his stance in this regard.

There are two kinds of composer: those who like to talk about their own works, and those who don't. Unfortunately I belong to the latter category. In my opinion the composer says everything through his music and nothing essential can be added by talking about it.

Form

Although not abundant, there are extant writings by Kokkonen about his compositions. A recurring theme, however, is about the organic process that underlies his works—comments that in many ways mirror Sibelius' own views of musical form. Consider, for instance, the following remarks from the above-cited essay on the third symphony:

The structure of the symphony [in general, not specifically the third symphony] has two distinct aspects: the "outer" and the "inner." By the "outer" structure I mean the way in which whole movements or major sections within movements are arranged in similar or contrasting blocks. The listener gains some impression of this "outer" structure at the first listening; it is primarily a matter of the interrelationship of entire movements of the work. In this respect the overall plans of my symphonies show a variable but basically constant principle: I tend to start and finish with slow movements, with relatively faster movements in between, sometimes only one, sometimes more ... I sometimes call this plan "biological," as in life too the most intensive period comes in the middle, not at the beginning or end.

I mentioned the "inner" structure of the symphony. By this I mean that a symphony develops from an extremely restricted number of motifs. These basic motifs are subject to continual metamorphosis; they grow, and appear in ever different combinations.

Composers thought symphonically before symphonies were ever composed, and this manner of thought will remain even though the pieces may not be called 'symphonies.' On the other hand, the forms in which the symphonic idea robs itself change with the passage of time. I have striven for expression of the organic, symphonic manner of thought and thus toward a personal solution of the problems thus caused. *Everything in a symphony depends on everything else.* [My emphasis]

Despite his rich comments, in several respects, Kokkonen's *Formenlehre* designs are quite traditional—namely, form is articulated by harmonic design and/or changes in orchestration, tempo, rhythm, etc. While ternary and rondo form both feature as important designs, sonata form also plays a significant role: the earliest instance of the design can be traced to his 1948 *Piano Trio* (each movement utilizes the form), and it plays a role in the other two pre-1957 chamber works. These works are characterized by relatively unambiguous tonal centers and formal demarcations. An interesting feature is the propensity for a movement to be structured using a mono-thematic design.

A new approach to sonata form begins to appear with the *Music for String Orchestra* from 1957. Specifically, there is a change to the underlying basis of a movement by the various large-scale deviations from "textbook" sonata *Formenlehre* structures, features that James Hepokoski has referred to as "sonata deformations."[2] Such structures are "in dialogue with the generic expectations of the sonata, even when some of the most important features of those expectations are not realized."[3] Although Hepokoski's following comment refers to Sibelius' post-fourth symphony works, it also has application with Kokkonen's works:

> [Sibelius strove] to create ad hoc musical structures that would be supported less by the horizon of expectations provided by the *Formenlehre* tradition than by the idiosyncratic, quasi-intuitive inner logic of the selected musical materials. Each major composition after the Fourth Symphony represents a relatively unmoored structural experiment that seeks its own course in uncharted formal waters.

Hepokoski has written at length about sonata deformations and their role in expanding the options of sonata form construction for nineteenth-century composers. For instance, in his book *Sibelius: Symphony No. 5*, he identifies five large categories of sonata deformations: (1) The Breakthrough Deformation; (2) The Introduction-Coda Frame; (3) Episodes within the Developmental Space; (4) Various Strophic/Sonata Hybrids; and (5) Multimovement Forms.[4] Space precludes a detailed examination of these various categories of deformations. However, one family of Strophic/Sonata Hybrid deformations that has relevance for the ensuing discussion surrounding Kokkonen's sonata forms is labeled "rotational form." This particular deformation describes a movement that cycles through the same thematic material several times, usually (but not always!)

in the same order. Hepokoski identifies this freer rotational/sonata-deformation approach as the underlying architecture of several works by such late nineteenth-century composers as Bruckner, Mahler, Strauss, and the later symphonic compositions of Sibelius. He defines rotational form as follows:

> Strictly considered, a rotational structure is more of a process than an architectural formula. In such a process ... [one] initially presents a relatively straightforward 'referential statement' of contrasting ideas. This is a series of differentiated figures, motives, themes, and so on ... which may be arranged to suggest such things, for example, as a sonata exposition. The referential statement may either cadence or recycles back through a transition to a second broad rotation. Second (and any subsequent) rotations normally rework all or most of the referential statement's material, which is now elastically treated. Portions may be omitted, merely alluded to, compressed, or, contrarily, expanded or even 'stopped' and reworked 'developmentally.' New material may also be added or generated. Each subsequent rotation may be heard as an intensified, meditative reflection on the material of the referential statement.[5]

By employing the process of rotational form, Kokkonen generated a variety of formal designs in his dodecaphonic compositions without the need of tonal centers to articulate tonal argument. Rather, a structure might deploy a series of differentiated thematic ideas, using different rhythmic motives and/or order positions from the same tone row, or even utilize different tone rows altogether, cast in a manner that suggests a series of events similar to a sonata form exposition. Subsequent rotations of the "exposition" manipulate the events; two common means by which Kokkonen typically modifies such thematic ideas are: (1) by altering the rhythmic profile of a thematic idea while retaining the integrity of the theme's pitch material, or (2) by permuting the order positions of a thematic idea while retaining, for the most part, its essential rhythmic profile. While the two compositional strategies are attractive in themselves, Kokkonen's penchant for utilizing multiple row orderings within a movement adds a further level of interest to a rotational structure. Specifically, different row orderings may be substituted for a particular theme in the various rotations. However, because he is careful to ensure a degree of intervallic and harmonic association between the various row orderings deployed in a movement, the end result is the simultaneous preservation of some core motivic element (i.e., the invariant pitches), with a sense of development upon the remaining features (i.e., the non-invariant portion of a row) between successive rotations.

Notes

1. Hako notes that this tune is a merger of four different folk hymns, and the version in the opera was probably never actually sung anywhere in real life. See Pekka Hako, *Finnish Opera*, p. 124.
2. A valuable exposition to Hepokoski's theory of sonata deformation is contained in James Hepokoski, *Sibelius: Symphony no. 5* (Cambridge: Cambridge University Press, 1993), chapter 3.
3. ibid, p. 5.
4. ibid, pp. 5–9.
5. ibid, p. 25.

Chapter 4

Symphonies

Symphony No. 1

Work on the first symphony began the same time as the String Quartet No. 1, although the latter was completed a year earlier than the symphony; it is scored for an orchestra of triple woodwinds and brass, along with a full complement of strings. The large number of motivic and contour relationships throughout the work makes it a remarkable achievement on many counts—a fact made even more impressive when one realizes that the symphony is, for all intent and purposes, Kokkonen's first extended composition for a full orchestra (the only large ensemble works that predate the symphony are the 1957 *Music for String Orchestra* and the orchestral song cycle *The Hades of the Birds*).

Kokkonen's first symphony appeared at an important moment in the development of Finnish music, for it demonstrated that one could satisfactorily marry (then) current modes of pitch construction with traditional formal genres such as the symphony, while using a compositional aesthetic of narrative structure reminiscent of Finland's greatest symphonist, Sibelius. The work, in other words, has been celebrated as one that is simultaneously modern and traditional. Needless to say, the critical success of the symphony significantly increased Kokkonen's prestige within the Finnish musical community: Kokkonen was placed at the forefront of a group of Finnish composers who had finally broken free of the shackles of Sibelius' musical dominance— namely, the nationalistic/romantic "trappings" that had plagued so many earlier Finnish composers during the prior four decades. (As was noted earlier, the remarkable success of Einar Englund's first two neoclassically styled symphonies from 1946 and 1948 had briefly placed him in an analogous position during the late 1940s; his influence, however, waned in the late 1950s as Englund had virtually ceased composing between 1955 and 1970, largely as a protest against what he believed were negative musical values represented by total serialism). In short, Kokkonen's symphony was immediately recognized as an important contribution to the symphonic repertoire and has continued to maintain an active life in the concert hall.

The first symphony was premiered on 15 March 1960; Paavo Berglund conducted the Finnish Radio Symphony Orchestra for the performance.

Movement One

All the pitch material in the first movement, marked *Moderato* ($\sharp$ = 76) is generated from one row ordering; only four row forms are used: the two primary row forms P_8 (I/A) and I_8 (I/B); and two secondary row forms I/C (P_1, i.e., the row form that is a T_5 transposition of row I/A) and I/D (I_1, i.e., the row form that is a T_5 transposition of row I/B). The four row forms are shown in Figure 4.1.

The movement is a two-rotation design, where the second rotation is a more extensively developed version of the first. The two rotations are preceded by a ternary-designed introduction; several of the motives that appear in this introduction recur prominently throughout the movement untransposed and with their contours unaltered. The outer sections of the ternary design (mm. 1–13 and 23–30) contain a pattern of three gestures (note that this three-gesture pattern appears twice in the A section (mm. 1–7 and 7–13) but only once in the A' section): (1) a fragment of rows I/A (for the A section) or I/B (for the A' section) is realized melodically by the low strings; (2) a passage of homophonic texture by the brass; and (3) an imitative passage played by the woodwinds. Figure 4.2 illustrates the opening three-gesture pattern in mm. 1–7. A contrasting middle section alters the pattern of gestures as follows: (1) a fragment of row I/B realized melodically by the oboe; (2) a melodic passage by the low strings; and (3) a homophonic passage played by the brass.

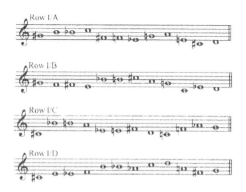

Figure 4.1 Row Forms of Symphony No. 1, mov. 1

Figure 4.2 Symphony No. 1, mov. 1, mm. 1–7

The movement proper begins at m. 31. The basis of rotation one's design is the simultaneous presentation of rows I/A and I/B, realized melodically by only the strings. As the strings rise steadily in register there is a gradual increase of rhythmic activity and density of texture by both the woodwinds and brass; the two families articulate many of the motives heard in the introduction, thereby forging formal associations in tandem with the textural development. The texture and dynamic level reach their maximum at m. 43; the point coincides with the apogee of the string melody. The remainder of rotation one, then, contains a gradual decrease in texture and dynamic level—changes that correspond with the registral descent by the strings' melodic material.

Rotation two begins at m. 61. Like rotation one, there is an increase in orchestral texture and dynamic level by the brass and woodwinds as the melodic material played by the strings ascends in register (as before, the strings unfold rows I/A and I/B simultaneously). One major divergence from the first rotation is that all the strings are used to build up the orchestral texture as preparation for the entrance of the other instrumental families; only two string parts were used in the analogous passage from rotation one. The culmination of rotation two occurs at m. 136, following which, as in rotation one, instruments are gradually removed from the orchestral texture as the strings decrease in register. However, an important deviation from rotation one is the greater number of the motives from the introduction that appear at this point, providing an understated sense of closure to the movement.

Movement Two

The intermezzo-like second movement is a ternary form. The row ordering from movement one remains; however, instead of P or I row forms, only retrograde row forms are utilized. The five specific row forms are shown in Figure 4.3: rows II/A and II/B are the retrograde forms of rows I/A and I/B, respectively; row II/C is the T_5 transposition of row II/A; and rows II/D and II/E are the T_5 and T_7 transpositions, respectively, of row II/B.

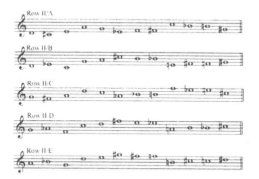

Figure 4.3 Row forms of Symphony No. 1, mov. 2

The opening part A contains three sections: mm. 1–11, 12–24, and 25–38; a closing passage in mm. 39–52 functions as a transition to the contrasting part B. Each of the three sections contains three similar gestures: (1) an opening passage in which the strings realize either row II/A or II/B in octaves and, notably, with a *pizzicato* articulation; (2) a melodic realization of row II/A played by the first violins (II/C is used in combination with row II/A in the second section); and (3) a number of repeated note patterns played by the brass and woodwinds, using pitch material based upon rows II/A, II/B and II/C.

Part B (mm. 52–67) is short in duration and distinguished by a completely different rhythmic profile. The design is essentially based upon two homophonic passages derived from row II/B; the passages are separated by a series of repeating sixteenth notes based upon the final four order positions of row II/C—i.e., F,E♭,E,C♯. Of note is the absence of row II/A.

Following a short transitional dialogue between the three flutes in mm. 68–78, part A' begins at m. 79. Like the earlier part A, there are three sections, although each now contains only two gestures instead of three: (1) an opening passage in which the strings project II/B in octaves and, as before, with a *pizzicato* articulation; and (2) an imitative passage in which all the rows are used. As regards this second gesture, in the first section (mm. 79–87) the imitation is between the three bassoons, in the second section (mm. 88–102) between the clarinets and the first bassoon, and in the section three (mm. 103–127) between all the brass. This latter gesture also contributes to the process generating the culminating passage of the movement as regards dynamic level, rhythmic activity and density of orchestral texture.

A two-part coda begins at m. 140. Part one is essentially an alternation between melodic realizations of row I/A played by different woodwind instruments and passages of *staccato*-articulated harmonies played by the strings and woodwinds combined together; the pitch material for these chords is obtained from row II/C. Part two of the coda begins at m. 160 and contains a series of imitative passages played by the strings, based upon the pitch material from row I/A.

Movement Three

The scherzo third movement, marked *Allegro*, is, like the second, a ternary form design. Six row forms, based upon the row ordering from movements one and two, are used. The rows are shown in Figure 4.4; the two most prevalent are III/A and III/B.

The opening part A is in two sections. The first section (mm. 1–29) contains several rhythmically vibrant presentations of row III/A by the unison strings, gestures that are answered by octave/unison presentations of rows III/A, III/B and III/C by the woodwinds. Figure 4.5 contains mm. 1–5 to illustrate the flavor of the rhythmic energy that pervades part A.

Section two begins at m. 30. The imitative nature between the strings and woodwinds from the opening section now changes to a texture where the two families coalesce into octave/unison statements of rows III/A and III/B; the brass in a constant eighth-note rhythm is now added as harmonic support. Importantly, the brass instruments state pitch material from a new row ordering: as Figure 4.6 illustrates, it is forged by taking every fifth pitch class from row III/A. The series of triadic harmonies that frequently harmonizes this new row ordering appears below the new row ordering. Initially, the triadic harmonies by the brass instruments appear at the rate of two chords per measures; further, each harmony is only played by the trumpet, horn, or trombone. At m. 38, however, the harmonic rhythm increases so that by m. 42, all the brass instruments are simultaneously heard (the textural crescendo that appears in mm. 40–42 is supported by an increase in dynamic level and an unmeasured tympani tremolo). A short transition played by the strings leads to part B, beginning at m. 57.

The series of triads introduced in part A is much more prominent in part B. For the most part, the harmonic rhythm of the repeating harmonic progression is one harmony per measure; the woodwinds, brass and strings are all used to orchestrate these chords. In section one of the tripartite-designed middle part (mm. 57–70) two row orderings are employed: P_1 by the first violins and the new row ordering III/G by the remainder of the orchestra. Section two is comprised of three imitative passages: (1) for woodwinds (mm. 71–79; rows III/A and III/B are used); (2) for the brass (mm. 80–89; rows III/A, III/B and III/C are used); and (3) for the woodwinds again (mm. 90–97; rows III/A and III/B are utilized). In section three, there is a lengthy imitative passage for the strings that contains several melodic realizations of the new row ordering.

The reappearance of the rhythmically aggressive unison string passage at m. 133 suggests a return to the opening part A. However, the passage is quickly abandoned, revealing a false reprise: instead, two further statements of the harmonic progression derived from the second row ordering appear between mm. 142 and 151.

Part A' proper begins at m. 152: unlike the opening part A, however, there is no interplay between the unison string passages and woodwinds. Instead, the entire A' part is one gradual increase in orchestral texture that culminates with the octave/unison statements by the woodwinds and strings of rows III/A and III/B (these statements begin at m. 185). Like the analogous passage from part A, these statements support the triadic harmonic progression that featured prominently in part B. The movement ends with the opening four triads from the progression, stated by the brass and played at a triple *forte* dynamic level; there is an *attacca* indication to the final movement.

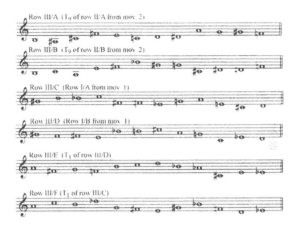

Figure 4.4 Row forms of Symphony No. 1, mov. 3

Figure 4.5 Symphony No. 1, mov. 3, mm. 1–5

Figure 4.6 New row ordering in Symphony No. 1, mov. 3

Movement Four

The rows used to generate the pitch material in the *adagio* fourth movement are shown in Figure 4.7. Row IV/B is the inversional row form of row IV/A that also begins on G♯. Row IV/C is a new row ordering: aside from its similar first order position of G♯, the row bears little similarity to rows IV/A or IV/B. However, row IV/C contains several relationships, as regards order position associations, with the primary row from the first three movements (i.e., rows I/A, II/A and III/A); this latter row is labeled IV/E. Finally, row IV/D is the inversional row form of IV/C that also begins on G♯.

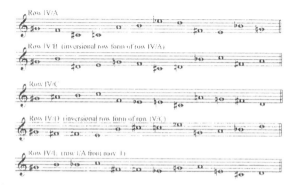

Figure 4.7 Row forms of Symphony No. 1, mov. 4

The row ordering introduced in the third movement is of primary import in the final movement: not only is the row melodically realized throughout, but the harmonic progression that realized the row in movement three is vital to generate the fourth movement's formal design— specifically, by alternating between the passages of imitative counterpoint involving a particular orchestral family and statements of the harmonic progression. However, with each recurrence of the chord progression, the orchestral texture and dynamic level increase, leading to the tutti climax of the movement in mm. 247–250. The design of the movement is shown in Table 4.1.

Table 4.1 Formal design of Symphony No. 1, mov. 4

Measure no.	Comments
205	Row IV/A in unison by strings; the triadic harmonic progression played by brass.
210	Rows IV/B and IV/C used as imitative counterpoint by the strings; the passage ends with statement of row IV/E by the strings.
217	Row IV/A is cast in a chorale texture by the brass.
220	Row IV/A is cast in a chorale texture by the brass.
224	Row IV/A realized as tetrachords, played by the strings, horns and flutes.
237	All five rows are realized within an imitative dialogue by the strings. The passage ends with an increase in dynamic level and register, leading to the climax of movement.
247	Row IV/A is realized in its characteristic harmonic progression; the entire orchestra is used for the passage.
253	The final measures are a coda. Here, imitative passages between the woodwinds and the strings are punctuated with twelve-note sonorities played by the entire orchestra. The work ends calmly with three repetitions of an E Major triad played at a *pianissimo* dynamic.

Symphony No. 2

Kokkonen's second symphony was written in 1961, one year following the first. It is the singular instance when two works of a similar genre from the composer's oeuvre were composed within such a close proximity of time. According to Kokkonen, there were ideas left unexplored from the compositional work on the first symphony that were significant enough to warrant putting aside other commissions and immediately begin work on another symphony. While Kokkonen's account is not implausible, it is more likely that the tremendous critical response his first symphony received was the motivating factor behind him composing a second symphony immediately after the first.

Like its companion piece, the pitch material of the second symphony is generated entirely from dodecaphonic procedures; by far the most common row form in the work is A♭,G,E,A,F♯,F,E♭,B♭,B,D,D♭,C. Figure 4.8 illustrates the P_8 row forms from the first and second symphonies (the row from the first symphony under discussion is the one utilized for the first and second movements, as well as the majority of the third). The similarity between the two rows does acknowledge several pitch associations between the two symphonies—for instance, the six invariant order positions (Ab,G,A,F,D and C)—at least with respect to these particular row forms. However, the relationship becomes weakened when one realizes that a limited number of rows is used in the first symphony (derived from, in total, three different row orderings), but that there are several important row forms employed in the second symphony and they are derived from the single row ordering used throughout the entire work.

Figure 4.8 Row forms of Symphony No. 2, mov. 1

The work is in four movements: the first and third movements are slow in tempo; the second and fourth are fast. The chronology of these movements as well as the *attacca* indication between the first and second movements and between the third and fourth movements suggests a bipartite interpretation of the work, a division further supported by the similar rotation-form designs of the first and third slow movements.

The second symphony received its premiere performance on 18 April 1961; Paavo Berglund conducted the Finnish Radio Symphony Orchestra for the performance.

Movement One

The opening movement is a three-rotation design (rotation two begins at m. 21; rotation three at m. 59); each rotation contains three sections. The first section emphasizes the strings, where the first violins play several successive realizations of a row (virtually always using the row forms P_8 or I_8): these violin melodies are supported by harmonies generated from rows shared among the remaining strings. As an illustration, Figure 4.9 contains the string passage in mm. 7–12 from rotation one: I_8 is stated by the first violins, while the remaining strings combined unfold P_7.

The second section of a rotation contains a series of harmonies played by the brass in chorale style; P_8 is the featured row form of these harmonic progressions. In addition, this section represents the loudest dynamic level of each rotation. In contrast to section two, section three is the most dynamically subdued and tranquil of each rotation. The woodwinds are featured in a dialogue of imitative counterpoint; inversional contours based upon both P and I row forms feature prominently among the lines.

Figure 4.9 Symphony No. 2, mov. 1, mm. 7–12

As is typical for movements in rotation-form design, each successive rotation expands upon the thematic and/or motivic ideas presented in rotation one. Consider, for instance, the alterations to section one between rotations one and three. In rotation one, there are only two rows used by the first violins in part one—P_8 in m. 1 and I_8 in m. 7; P_8 is shared among the other strings for the first row realization and P_7 for the second realization. However, in rotation three (mm. 59–74) the number of row forms increases to four (all are again stated by the first violins). Further, the first violins explore a higher register for a much greater duration. There are also notable alterations associated with the strings accompanying the first violins' melodies: while each of the two rows stated by the first violins in rotation one is supported by a single row shared among the remaining strings, in rotation three there are typically two different row forms shared among the strings supporting each of the first violin row statements. Further, the rhythmic activity of the supporting string lines and the dynamic level both increase (from *piano* in rotation one to *fortissimo* in rotation three).

One further comment as regards the rotational design of the movement is warranted—specifically, the sequential ordering of the three sections from rotation to rotation. In rotation one, the brass chorale section follows the imitative woodwind dialogue. However for the remainder of the movement, the two sections are reversed and the woodwind dialogue is the final feature of each rotation.

Movement Two

As was noted above, the ternary-form second movement follows the first without pause. Part A contains two sections. Aside from the opening eight measures where the cellos and double basses double the bassoon and contra-bassoon lines (mm. 105–112), part A is devoid of strings. Essentially, the first section contains a series of statements of different row forms, each realized by a different member of the woodwind family; the end of each row statement is punctuated by a short series of chords played by the brass. The first section overall ends with a succession of brass chords in mm. 130–135 played at a *forte* dynamic; the chords are preceded by a statement of I_8 in mm. 127–130 played by the three trombones. Measures 123–134 are illustrated in Figure 4.10; the row form and contour of the trombone gesture in mm. 127–130 recur throughout the movement.

The second section of part A begins at m. 135: aside from a brief octave/unison realization of RP_8 by the woodwinds in mm. 137–140, the section is exclusively associated with the brass. Five-note fragments from different row forms are used as ostinatos, while a gradual crescendo supports a second marked statement of I_8 in mm. 153–160, again realized with the same contour as in mm. 127–130, but now played in unison by all four horns and the first trombone. The tremendous dramatic energy that ends part A is dissipated by the transition to part B (mm. 160–179), a passage wherein an octave/unison melodic statement of P_9 is played in long rhythmic values by all the strings and woodwinds.

Part B is quite short (mm. 180–194) and distinguished by its orchestration for strings only at a *piano* dynamic level. The texture is reminiscent of the melody and accompaniment that typified section one from each rotation in movement one: the first violins play statements of the row form RP_8 and are supported by several realizations of row form RP_9 shared among the remaining strings.

Part A' begins at m. 195 and contains two sections. Like part A, the woodwinds play a series of different row forms (occasionally doubled by the trumpet). However, there are two notable differences between the present passage and the analogous section from part A: (1) the absence of the brass chords to punctuate the row statements; and (2) the increased energy generated by the extensive sixteenth-note rhythmic activity by the strings. Section two, like its analogue from part A, is distinguished by numerous ostinatos generating a gradual dynamic crescendo that leads to the cadential gesture at m. 258 of a series of uni-rhythm brass chords. However, while the ostinatos from part A were produced from the continuous repetition of five-note row fragments, they are formed by a series of three- and four-note row fragments.

Figure 4.10 Symphony No. 2, mov. 2, mm. 123–136

Although the series of brass chords at m. 258 suggests a cadential gesture analogous with m. 159 from part A, the horn melody in mm. 255–257 (i.e., the melody preceding the chords in m. 259) has a different contour and is not derived from the I_8 row form, the one heard at the similar moment in part A. The absence of the two elements that characterized the ending of part A provides a link to an expanded development section in mm. 259–300, one where the ostinatos by the brass and woodwinds support statements of several different row forms by the strings. Ultimately, however, the primary melodic material is transferred to the horns and at mm. 296–300 we finally hear a statement of I_8 by the brass in its characteristic contour (i.e., as in Figure 4.10). Like part A, the intense energy in mm. 296–300 is immediately dissipated, leading to a short coda.

The movement ends quietly with a *Klangfarben* realization of I_8 by the woodwinds.

Movement Three

Like the first, movement three is slow in tempo. The form is a two-rotation design (the second rotation begins at m. 47); each rotation contains two sections. Section one is characterized by interaction between the woodwinds and strings, where row statements are, for the most part, realized in a *Klangfarben* manner. In short, section one is distinguished by a rich mosaic of motives and an interesting kaleidoscope of colours. By contrast, section two features the strings with extensive legato lines. The melodic emphasis is largely placed upon the first violins: the expanded lines are generated from successive, complete statements of different row forms. The remaining strings play a supporting role for the first violins: at certain points a row form is shared among the other strings; during other passages, different row forms are realized by each string part.

Each rotation ends with similar two-part cadential gestures. The first portion contains a series of harmonies played by the brass; the second is a transitional melody with a descending contour. The cadential gesture is extensively developed in the second rotation, engendering a greater degree of tension at the end of the movement: for instance, both gestures increase in dynamic level and orchestral texture; further, the transitional melody becomes more rhythmically complex.

The movement ends with a repetition of the series of harmonies from the two-part cadential gesture; the final sonority is sustained and provides a link to the final movement.

Movement Four

The short final movement, marked *Allegro vivace*, is cast in a crescendo-form design—namely, there is a gradual, uni-directional increase in dynamic level and density of orchestral texture as the movement unfolds. The two brass melodies shown in Figure 4.11 feature prominently throughout the movement: melody X is played only by the trumpets and is generated from a seven-note fragment of a RP_8 row form; melody Y is played solely by the horns and forged from a fragment of RI_{10}.

The pattern to the appearance of the two melodies provides the underlying strategy of the large-scale crescendo: as the movement unfolds, the duration separating them decreases, generating a subtle contribution to the overall drama. The process of this continuous decrease in length between the two events reaches its goal in mm. 204–215 when both melodies are simultaneously presented; the moment corresponds with the convergence of maximum dynamic level and orchestral texture and leads to the sustained octave/unison pitch A in mm. 216–221.

Figure 4.11 Two melodic gestures in Symphony No. 2, mov. 4

The character of the movement shifts abruptly with the short coda beginning at m. 222: the orchestral texture is sparse, and the dynamic level and tempo decrease dramatically to *piano* and *Poco più lento*. The coda consists of three gestures: (1) the series of harmonies from the cadential gestures in movement three which appear in mm. 225–230; (2) a passage of imitative counterpoint played by the woodwinds, reminiscent of the woodwind dialogue from section three that ended each rotation in movement one (the passage is contained in mm. 232–238); and (3) a passage solely for the strings in which the first violins present a realization of the P_8 row form and the remaining strings unfold a statement of P_4 that supports the first violins' melody (the passage is very suggestive of section two from each of the rotations in movement three). The movement ends quietly with a sustained twelve-note sonority played by the entire orchestra.

Symphony No. 3

Kokkonen's third symphony, written in 1967, represented a new compositional approach, one that characterized virtually every work from the remainder of his oeuvre. Specifically, although dodecaphonic procedures remained the primary means by which these later compositions were structured, tertian harmonies became utilized to a greater degree with these dodecaphonic configurations, thus increasing the pitch resources of a piece. The tertian sonorities in these works, however, are virtually always non-functional from a traditional tonal perspective—rather, any sense of tonal focus is through repetition of a particular sonority or through the assertion of some type of neighbor-note or neighbor-harmony. As an example, consider a prevalent septachord in movement one from the symphony—{E♭,F♯,G,A,B♭,C,D}. Although the twelve-tone rows used in the movement will be discussed shortly, this particular seven-element set proves vital as it is frequently partitioned into two smaller tertian sonorities—an E♭ Major triad and a dominant seventh chord built on D ({D,F♯,A,C}; typically, it is situated higher in register than the E♭ Major triad). The complementary pitch-class set is the pentachord {E,F,G♯,B,C♯}. Important here is the E,G♯,B triad from the pentachord: the triad is often in proximity to the D-Dominant 7th/E♭ Major chord complex, in a sense, competing with the semitone-related chord complex.

Although cast in four movements, Kokkonen described the symphony in terms of a three-movement work, one where the first movement is an extensive introduction to the work as a whole. From this perspective, then, the second movement is not a scherzo but, rather, the main allegro of the symphony; the third movement is the intermezzo; and the *Adagio* combines elements of a finale and a slow movement.

The work is scored for the largest-sized orchestra Kokkonen ever used: in addition to the normal complement of strings, there are triple woodwinds and brass, piano, celesta, harp and a battery of percussion instruments. The symphony was first performed on 12 September 1967 for the fortieth anniversary concert of the Finnish Radio Symphony Orchestra; Paavo Berglund conducted the orchestra for the performance. The critical success of the symphony was immediate, and in 1968 Kokkonen received the Nordic Council's Music Award for the composition.

Movement One

The three row orderings in Figure 4.12 account for a large percentage of the pitch material in the movement. Four row forms represent the six-note row I/A: P_3, P_9, P_{10} and I_{10}; P_{10}, i.e., the illustrated row form, is the most prevalent. Row I/B is essentially two different series of five harmonic dyads, labeled harmonic series no.1 and no. 2. The six-element row I/C is a linear reordering of the first three harmonic dyads from the first harmonic series of row I/B.

As described above, the movement opens with the seven-note chord {E♭,F♯,G,A,B♭,C,D}; its initial occurrence is played by the harp in mm. 1–2 as a G harmonic minor scale beginning on scale degree six (E♭). Although the septachord does not return in this particular linear fashion, there are numerous "harmonic" occurrences of the sonority throughout the movement. More important, however, are the tertian sonorities that Kokkonen extracts from the septachord—namely, the dominant 7th chord built on the D and E♭ Major triad described above. An E Major triad is also consistently associated with the D7th/E♭ Major complex, adding a further harmonic relationship with the "bitonal" sonority; for instance, the triad is present during the opening measures, supporting the opening G minor scale.

Figure 4.12 Row forms of Symphony No. 3, mov. 1

The tripartite-designed movement proper begins at m. 9. In the first part, mm. 9–24, all the primary rows of the movement are introduced. The strings dominate, with the woodwinds used occasionally for contrast; Figure 4.13 illustrates a typical series of realizations of the three rows in mm. 9–14 from part A: row I/A is realized by the first violin in m. 9 and mm. 11–12, second violin in m. 10 and mm. 12–13, piccolo in mm. 10–11, and the three woodwinds in m. 14; row I/B is realized by the woodwinds in m. 9; and row I/C is realized by the first violin in mm. 10–11 and 12–14, the second violin in m. 11, and the woodwinds in m. 14.

A transition begins at m. 24, in which the strings and low woodwinds present a sustained harmonic version of the opening septachord and the piano arpeggiates the E♭ Major/D 7th/E Major complex. The passage ends with a series of piano chords in mm. 28–29 played triple *forte*.

The most extensive development takes place in the second part of the movement (mm. 30–45). This part is structured by successive realizations of rows I/A and I/B, punctuated repeatedly by the two series of harmonic dyads of row I/B cast in a variety of orchestrations. The lowest register of the cellos and double basses is employed at the outset; with successive statements of the various rows, there is a gradual ascent in register through the use of the violas and violins. Associated with this rise in register, however, is an enlarged orchestral texture through the steady addition of the remaining orchestral families—a systematic process that culminates with the *fortissimo* tutti chord in m. 45. A short transition (mm. 46–53) returns to the lowest string register and segues to the third and final part of the movement. Here, the interaction between the P_3, P_{10} and P_{11} row forms appears one final time: an ostinato constructed from a harmonic version of P_3, played by the low woodwinds and strings, horns, trombones and piano (all in their lowest respective registers) in quarter-note rhythm pervades this short section (mm. 54–60); realizations of P_{10} and P_9 in contrasting thirty-second-note rhythms are played by solo woodwinds over the top of the ostinato. The movement ends with tutti chord played *mezzo-forte*, orchestrated to articulate the E♭ Major/D 7th/E Major complex.

Movement Two

The *Allegro* second movement is a ternary form. With five different row orderings (shown in Figure 4.14), the movement is more harmonically complex than the first. Of note is that row II/D is virtually always realized harmonically and in the particular registral spacing illustrated, as opposed to the remaining rows, which are equally realized both melodically and harmonically. There are several harmonic associations between these rows. For instance, the first four, seventh and eighth order positions from row II/C are invariant with the uppermost four, and second and third lowest pitches of row II/D. In other words, the two rows are similar, but in different dimensions (i.e., row II/C is melodic, whereas row II/D is harmonic). The upshot to such pitch associations is that these rows are more closely related than their apparent differences might at first suggest and, therefore, engender a subtle sense of harmonic unity to the movement.

Part A essentially contains interplay between members of different orchestral families using five-, six-, or seven-note fragments of rows II/A and II/B, punctuated with repetitions of the harmonic sonorities from row II/D. An underlying *crescendo*, as regards orchestral density and dynamic level, underscores the constant interchange and culminates with the triple *forte* orchestral tutti in mm. 37–40.

Part B begins at m. 49 following a ten-measure transition dominated by row II/D. It opens with a whimsical, capricious styled realization of row II/C: this particular realization of the row appears in virtually every measure from this portion of the movement and plays a vital role in shaping the character of part B. The passage from mm. 82–89 represents the culmination of part B, where five repeated tutti chords, utilizing all eight pitches of row II/D, are played by the entire orchestra. Amidst these repeating sonorities, all four horns play the P_3 row form of row I/A at a *fortissimo* dynamic level, creating a brief association with the opening movement at this key moment.

Figure 4.13 Symphony No. 3, mov. 1, mm. 9–14

Figure 4.14 Row forms of Symphony No. 3, mov. 2

Part A' begins at m. 93. The harmonic basis of this final part is a series of perfect fifth dyads that repeat constantly as a type of chaconne. Over the top of the dyad series are numerous successive realizations of five- to seven-note fragments of rows II/A and II/B. As with part A, an underlying *crescendo*, as regards orchestral density and dynamic level, underscores the constant interchange between the two rows and culminates with the triple *forte* orchestral tutti in mm. 128–130.

A short coda begins immediately at m. 131 and recapitulates all the prominent motives from the movement used to realize rows II/A, II/B and II/C; they are cast in a whimsical manner reminiscent of part B.

Movement Three

The third movement, marked *Allegretto moderato*, is also a ternary form. There are two harmonic resources that generate virtually all the pitch material of the movement. The first is the three rows illustrated in Figure 4.15: row III/B is the inversional row form of row III/A that begins on the pitch B, while row III/C is a transposed version of row III/A beginning on the pitch F♯. The second harmonic resource is a type of tonal centricity where a pitch is reinforced via melodic motion (typically chromatic) surrounding a particular pitch; the most prevalent tonal centers are the pitches D and A. Figure 4.16 illustrates both harmonic processes at work in mm. 10–13: the flute unfolds a realization of P_{11} while supported by the oboe's and violin's chromatic motion surrounding both D and A.

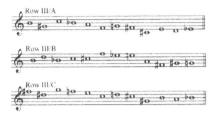

Figure 4.15 Row forms of Symphony No. 3, mov. 3

Figure 4.16 Symphony No. 3, mov. 3, mm. 10–13

Part B (mm. 28–55) is characterized by dramatic changes to both the rhythm and harmony established in part A. Specifically, there is an increase in rhythmic activity from the pervasive triplet sixteenth-note figures supporting the various row realizations. However, even the statements of row III/A and III/B are altered rhythmically: the combination of sixteenth- and thirty second-note figures adds a capricious quality to these melodic realizations. As regards harmony, the harmonic support for the various realizations of rows III/A and III/B increases from the melodic motion of two voices surrounding a tonal center to four-voice sonorities;

perfect fifth dyads play a prominent role in the vast majority of these harmonies.

A short transition between m. 49 and m. 55 features a short four-voice chorale-styled series of harmonies played by the trumpets and first trombone; once again, perfect fifth dyads play an important function in these harmonies. The contour and rhythm of rows III/A and III/B from part A return in part A'; however, they are now cast within a more imitative and dense, albeit dynamically subdued, texture. The movement ends quietly with six repetitions of a D Major triad that includes an added pitch E, set at a dynamic level of *pianissimo*.

Movement Four

Figure 4.17 illustrates the primary rows that are used in the final *Adagio* movement. Rows IV/A, IV/B and IV/C are all related to one another: IV/B is inversionally related to row IV/A, while IV/C is a T_7 transposition of row IV/B (it should be noted that row IV/C is frequently realized as the series of harmonic dyads illustrated in the fourth system). The three rows are all related to the primary row from movement two, row II/A—in fact, the first six pitches of row IV/C are identical with the first six of row II/A. In addition, row IV/D is identical to row I/D from movement one. In short, the extensive use of these four rows is an important means by which Kokkonen forges a number of harmonic associations, both within the final movement and across the work as a whole. Row IV/E is the one other row used in the movement: the row is used minimally (it only appears three times within the opening measures) and, thus, will garner no further discussion.

The movement is an interesting tripartite design that contains a rich mosaic of themes, not only between realizations of the rows just identified, but also between themes from the other three movements, thus engendering a summary-like quality to the movement. Part one (mm. 1–19) is characterized by extensive trills by the strings, tympani and bass drum that support melodic realizations of portions from rows IV/A, IV/E and, most frequently, IV/B. The first four or five pitches from each row are used for all these statements, which are cast in either sixteenth-note or sextuplet sixteenth-note rhythms. A *crescendo* design underlies the first part: along with the greater frequency of these row fragments is a greater harmonic density derived from the gradual augmented number of instruments playing unmeasured tremolos and trills, as well as a general overall increase in dynamic level. For instance, the movement begins with only the strings playing a realization of the first six pitches from row IV/A in unmeasured tremolos at a dynamic level of *pianissimo*. However, by m. 19 the dynamic level has increased to triple *forte* and all the instruments of the orchestra are involved in the tutti harmony.

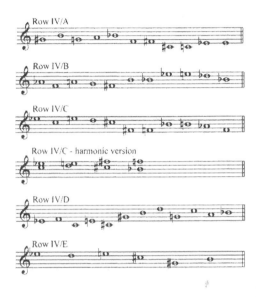

Figure 4.17 Row forms of Symphony No. 3, mov. 4

Part two begins at m. 20 and returns to the opening *pianissimo* dynamic level. This portion of the movement begins with a dialogue between different solo woodwind and brass instruments using melodic material derived from rows IV/B and IV/C; the strings support this discourse. At m. 29, however, there is a shift from solo instruments to an exchange between the violins and horns; further, the melodic material upon which the interaction is based is now primarily from rows IV/A and IV/C. There is a general increase in orchestral texture (albeit for strings only) and dynamic level to *fortissimo* (in m. 34)—although both parameters are less when compared with the ending of part A (recall from the preceding paragraph that the dynamic level reached triple *forte* and utilized the entire orchestra).

Once again, the dynamic level returns to a *pianissimo* level to initiate the third and final part of the movement; like the other two parts, there is a concomitant gradual increase in orchestral texture associated with the dynamic *crescendo* that culminates with the triple *forte* in the final measures of the movement. What makes the final part particularly impressive, however, is the masterful recapitulation of not only the major thematic material associated with the rows from the fourth movement, but also ideas from earlier movements. For instance, row I/A from movement one subtly appears at a *pianissimo* dynamic level by the oboe in m. 43; the theme becomes increasingly prominent and culminates with the trombone statement in mm. 66–67, leading to the triple *forte* E Major triad played by the brass in m. 67. A second example involves row IV/C: harmonic dyads begin to appear near the outset of part three and are used as harmonic support for the solo themes that appear successively. At m. 48, however, the three-chord E♭ Major/D 7th/E Major complex from movement one begins to be substituted as harmonic support for the numerous melodic motives and increasingly dominates the musical fabric towards the end of the movement. In fact, the final sonority itself recalls associations with the ending of the first movement: although the registral spacing of the two chords is different, both are orchestrated in such a manner that the three triads are perceived within the tutti chord.

Symphony No. 4

Kokkonen's final symphony was commissioned for a commemorative concert on 16 November 1971 to celebrate the composer's fiftieth birthday. As with the prior three symphonies, the premiere was given by the Finnish Radio Symphony Orchestra and conducted by one of Kokkonen's most ardent champions, Paavo Berglund. The work was immediately heralded as a masterpiece and has become the most performed and celebrated of his four symphonies.

Although the dimension and scope of the fourth symphony are significantly greater than the *Symphonic Sketches* of 1968, the two works share similarities as regards formal designs—namely, an arch-form design of moderate tempo for the first movement, a ternary-designed scherzo middle movement and a rotation-form-designed *adagio* finale. While the formal similarities of the earlier work suggest that the *Symphonic Sketches* may have been a model for the symphony from three years later, the pitch structure—i.e., the design of the row orderings and realization of the rows—and parameters such as rhythm and orchestration are so significantly different that, in the end, only general comparisons are applicable.

The unusual number of movements is worthy of reflection, a position upon which Kokkonen himself took great pains to comment (in point of fact, there is only a handful of three-movement instrumental works throughout Kokkonen's oeuvre). Consider, for instance his comments about the work's design in the program notes from the premiere performance:

> In the composition of a symphony the overall architectural design is of central importance. I have always found it more natural to begin and end with movements in a relatively slow tempo and put the fast movements in the middle. This formal principle, the reverse of the classical order, seemed to correspond best to the concept of the symphony as a product of organic growth towards which I have aspired. This macrostructure is repeated in various forms in almost all of my symphonic works. It was part of the original plan to conclude the fourth symphony with a fast movement that would grow out of the preceding adagio. A good half of the time I devoted to this symphony was spent on developing this idea—an idea which in the end was never realized. I could not get the allegro to "sit" as a continuation of the adagio and I could not create the balance for which I was striving. The final outcome was the discovery that the material I had intended as the finale to the symphony fitted, in shortened and revised form, the ending of the second movement. The symphony thus came to consist of three movements: moderato—allegro—adagio. Since all the elements of a symphony are interdependent, this meant that the whole process of composition had to be begun again from the beginning. Once the overall design had become clear, however, the actual process of writing proceeded fairly quickly.

Several commentators have suggested that the harmonic language of the fourth symphony is governed by tertian-styled triads; in other words, it is representative of compositions from Kokkonen's later period that are typically labeled as freely tonal or neoromantic. While it cannot be denied that tertian sonorities are vital to one's aural experience of the symphony, analysis illuminates that the pervasive use of dodecaphonic procedures makes it more appropriate to view the work as structured by a composite of different harmonic resources—one in which tertian sonorities certainly play a role, albeit more supportive in function when compared with the work's many twelve-tone structures.

Movement One

The two row orderings that generate the majority of the pitch material of the movement are illustrated in Figure 4.18. Two row forms represent the first row ordering and are labeled rows I/A and I/B for the prime and inverted forms shown (retrograde versions of these row forms are also occasionally used). Rows I/A and I/B are only used melodically; virtually all the harmonies in the movement are derived from the second row ordering—i.e., row I/C. However, while the ordering of the pitches in the "melodic" rows I/A and I/B is quite strict, the treatment of the dyads of row I/C is relatively free: repetitions, inversions and reorderings of these dyads occur and by combining these procedures with different rhythmic patterns, orchestrations and registers, Kokkonen generates a variety of harmonic progressions based upon essentially very simple means.

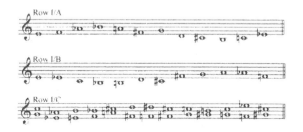

Figure 4.18 Row forms of Symphony No. 4, mov. 1

The movement opens calmly: a sustained pitch E supports a dialogue between the woodwinds of various realizations of row I/C; Figure 4.19 illustrates these features during the opening few measures. However, harmonic ambiguity over the centricity of the pitch E is generated by the numerous shifts to the C♯-G♯ dyad placed in a low register; the harmonic change frequently punctuates phrases, acting as a type of cadential gesture (the first such cadential gesture occurs in mm. 6–9). At m. 26 there is a change in orchestration: row I/C now shifts to the strings (and briefly by the harp in mm. 33–36); the woodwinds now realize row I/A. The C♯-G♯ dyad in m. 42 demarcates two new events: (1) for the first time, row I/B is given equal status along with row I/A (both are played by the violins); and (2) row I/C is absent for a few measures, primarily to increase attention upon the strings at this point. By m. 51, however, row I/C again dominates the musical landscape, only now versions of the row are simultaneously stated by both the strings and woodwinds.

The next major section of the movement begins at m. 63. The melodic focus is now almost entirely upon the violins playing realizations of row I/B; row I/C is played by the lower strings, brass, woodwinds and percussion and supports numerous statements of row I/B.

The violins begin the section in their lowest tessitura and gradually ascend in register, leading to mm. 83–92, the culminating passage of the movement, both in terms of orchestral density and dynamic level. Of note is that a third pitch is added to row III/C during this passage, generating a series of tertian harmonies. Following a brief transitional passage for the strings alone, the final section begins at m. 102. Like the opening, the emphasis is almost entirely upon statements of row I/C played at a *piano* dynamic level. Although the C♯-G♯ dyad appears occasionally, the movement ends as it began—calmly, with an E pedal at a *pianissimo* dynamic level. Interestingly, however, the final E Major harmony of the movement is "muddied" through the addition of a C minor triad. As we shall come to see, the {E,G♯,B/C,E♭,G} hexachord has significance in the final movement.

Figure 4.19 Symphony No. 4, mov. 1, mm. 1–9

Figure 4.19, continued

Movement Two

The ternary-designed second movement, marked *Allegro*, is a scherzo in
the true sense of the term—one suffused with whim and humor, brought
about largely from a kaleidoscope of orchestral colours, dynamics, rhythms

and textures. It is scored for the largest number of percussion instruments in the work—eight (only the vibraphone is absent).

There are essentially three categories of pitch material in the movement. The first is the four twelve-tone rows shown in Figure 4.20 (there are three different row orderings; rows II/A and II/B are retrograde versions of each other). An interesting attribute of the realization of the second row ordering (i.e., row II/C), as regards rhythm, is that the first pitch, F, is always articulated three times before the second order position appears. While the first three rows appear both melodically and harmonically, row II/D, like row I/C from movement one, contains a series of harmonic dyads that is somewhat free in the ordering of its constituent elements. Contrasting with the four rows (which, it should be noted, generate a significant percentage of the pitch material in the movement) are two other categories of pitch material, both of which are used almost exclusively for scalar passages: (1) the octatonic collection; and (2) sequential passages based upon order positions 2–5 from row II/C (an example of such a scalar passage, for instance, would be E,G,A♭,B♭-A,C,C♯,D♯-D,F,F♯,G♯).

Both of the outer parts of the scherzo contain two sections. The first is distinguished by a rather frenetic presentation of the pitch materials identified in the previous paragraph: *Klangfarben*-like realizations of the four rows abound, while frequent attacks by the temple blocks, xylophone, harp, or suspended cymbal punctuate particular pitches, creating syncopated rhythms that increase the frenzied nature of the musical materials. Although the rapid succession of row statements in the second section (these sections begin at m. 53 and m. 159 of parts A and A', respectively) continues the frantic presentation of the music materials that characterized the first, they are virtually always confined to a particular instrument or doubled at the octave/unison with other instruments—in short, *Klangfarbenmelodie* plays a much less significant role. Further, unlike the constant shift of registers that typified the row statements in section one, there is a gradual, progressive increase in registral expanse that corresponds with the succession of row statements in the second section: both parts A and A' culminate with a statement of row II/B played by the violins in their upper register, followed by a series of tutti chords that function as cadential gestures. Further, along with the systematic progression of row statements is a concomitant increase of orchestral texture, notably the tertian-styled triads that harmonize the various melodic fragments played by the woodwinds and brass.

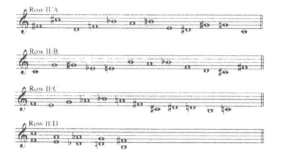

Figure 4.20 Row forms of Symphony No. 4, mov. 2

Part B of the movement (mm. 92–125) is itself a ternary design: the outer sections emphasize the strings and contain realizations of rows II/A and II/B in somewhat long rhythmic values (row II/C is also occasionally used by the woodwinds and cast in short rhythmic values). By contrast, the brief middle section (mm. 102–107) presents realizations of row II/D by the flutes and strings in long rhythmic values; of note is the complete absence of the brass.

Movement Three

The pitch material of the final movement, marked *Adagio*, is primarily based upon the three row orderings shown in Figure 4.21. Rows II/A and II/B are inversionally related row forms that represent the first row ordering. The two rows are treated somewhat freely in that all eleven pitches from a row may be stated, or hexachords from the rows may be combined. However, aside from the *Klangfarben* styled introduction in mm. 1–8, these two rows are always confined to either a single instrument or a group of instruments as an octave/unison statement. The second row ordering, row III/C, is a series of harmonic dyads. Like the prior two movements, there is freedom in the realization of such a series of dyads. Further, the harmonic dyads act frequently as harmonic support for the various melodic statements of rows III/A and III/B—in effect, there is often two simultaneous harmonic layers. The final row ordering (labeled row III/D) is only melodically realized; further, unlike rows III/A and III/B, row III/D is always realized in its entirety.

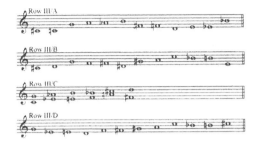

Figure 4.21 Row forms of Symphony No. 4, mov. 3

The movement is a two-rotation design, with a brief introduction and coda; each rotation contains three sections. Section one is characterized by either complete, or hexachordal statements, of rows III/A and III/B, played by the woodwinds and strings. For the most part, these row statements are harmonically supported by realizations of the dyads from row III/C. Section two is predominantly homophonic in texture and is distinguished by numerous repetitions of a hexachord generated by combining C minor and E Major triads, in a rhythm of nine sixteenths per two quarter notes (as was identified earlier, the hexachord that ends movement one is derived from the same two triads). Of note is the vital role the brass plays in this section. The dramatic quality of these chords is intensified by the addition of the octave/unison statements of row III/A, played by the woodwinds and violins near the end of the section. Melodic realizations of row III/D, played by the strings, dominate section three. The section culminates with a series of cadential harmonies; once again the sonorities are hexachords generated by combining C minor and E Major triads together.

As is typical for a movement structured in a rotation design, the second rotation elaborates the material presented in rotation one. For instance, in the first section of rotation two, there is a greater number of statements of rows III/A and III/B and a more pervasive use of row III/C than in rotation one. Section two not only is slightly longer in duration in rotation two, but the repetitions of the C minor/E Major hexachord encompass a larger number of instruments and a greater dynamic level. Finally, the successive octave/unison statements of row III/D by the violins, violas and cellos in section three of rotation two—there is a gradual augmentation in dynamic level and register with each successive statement—engender a greater sense of tension (one that subtly prepares the listener for the explosive chords that end the movement in mm. 94–96), when compared with the analogous passage in rotation one, where only the first violins play one statement of row III/D and in the instrument's lower register.

Chapter 5

Orchestral Works

Music for String Orchestra

The four-movement *Music for String Orchestra* dates from 1957 and represents Kokkonen's first orchestral composition following nearly two decades of piano, voice and piano and chamber works. The work has at times been labeled *Music for Strings*, a title that Kokkonen was quick to admonish, for he was explicit that the normal complement of strings from a symphony orchestra, and not a string quartet or the reduced forces of a chamber ensemble is the appropriate size of ensemble for the work. His insistence of the orchestral string ensemble should not be seen as some pedantic stance; rather, Kokkonen, more any anyone would have recognized the importance that the *Music for String Orchestra* would have played in his development as a composer—namely, as a move away from the intimate nature of solo and chamber music to the realm of symphonic music for which he is so celebrated. Given the fame that the first two symphonies brought him, it seems hardly surprising that Kokkonen would have situated the *Music for String Orchestra* more closely with these more substantial works that appeared not long after, rather than his chamber works from the 1950s.

The *Music for String Orchestra* also represents an important evolutionary stage away from the tonally based neoclassical-styled works from the prior twenty years and the dodecaphonically-styled works that characterize the vast majority of Kokkonen's works after 1957. While not every movement utilizes tone rows (only the first and third movements contain tone rows; the second and fourth do not), there is a similarity of compositional approach in all four movements. Specifically, regardless of whether a movement is structured by row orderings, or instead by simply a small number of motives, the pitch material is rarely transposed. To avoid monotony, then, one engenders symphonic argument more from engaging these rows or motives with a variety of rhythms, imitative procedures, textures and registral changes rather than by developing specific attributes of the pitch material itself.

The *Music for String Orchestra* was premiered on 5 March 1957 by the string section of the Finnish Radio Symphony Orchestra; Nils-Eric

Fougstedt conducted the ensemble. As was identified earlier, Paavo
Berglund was the concert master of the Finnish Radio Symphony Orchestra
at that time. Kokkonen and Berglund stuck up an immediate friendship,
one that had lifelong professional consequence, as Berglund premiered
virtually every remaining orchestra work by Kokkonen and championed his
music, both within Finland and abroad.

Movement One

What is perhaps the most striking aspect of the first movement is not the
different number of row orderings—five—but rather, that an unusual
stylistic feature that characterized so many of Kokkonen's dodecaphonic
works appeared very early in his forays into twelve-tone composition.
Figure 5.1 illustrates the five different twelve-tone row orderings used in
the movement. While rows I/B through I/E only employ a single row form,
there are several row forms of row I/A. There are no clear formal
demarcations in the movement; instead, realizations of the five twelve-tone
orderings interact with each other in various ways, and it is the
evolutionary nature of these row combinations that generates the three-
rotation design of the movement.

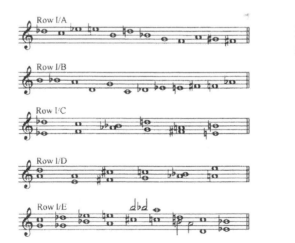

Figure 5.1 Row forms of *Music for String Orchestra*, mov. 1

There are six identifiable sections in rotation one. The first (mm. 1–
32) opens with contrapuntal imitation between rows I/A and I/B (Figure 5.2
illustrates such a dialogue between the celli and violas in mm. 1–7).

Figure 5.2 *Music for String Orchestra*, mov. 1, mm. 1–10

Section two begins at m. 33. Here, the "harmonic" rows I/C and I/D (row I/C appears only minimally in a melodic realization and row I/D never does) are played by the first violins and separated, at minimum, by a measure of silence between entrances. Further, row I/A is absent and row I/B appears only once and in long rhythmic values.

The third section begins at m. 52 and is characterized by an increased interaction between rows I/C and I/D (now played by the second violins and violas); for the most part, the two rows appear in alternate measures. The first violins now play a realization of row I/B in a higher register than heard previously.

Section four begins at m. 68. Like the prior section, there is interaction between rows I/C and I/D, combined with row I/A played by the first violins. The harmonically oriented row I/E appears for the first time.

An interesting new section begins at m. 86: only rows I/C and I/D are used and segregated between different instruments for the first time (further, row I/C is used melodically for the first time, specifically in mm. 99—112 by the celli and double basses and mm. 121–133 by the first violins).

The final section of part one begins at m. 140. Like section five, rows I/A and I/B are absent—however, rows I/C and I/D are simultaneously stated for the first time with identical rhythmic values. Essentially, the section is characterized by the interaction between statements of the rows I/C-I/D complex and row I/E.

Rotation two begins at m. 177; the original realization and tempo of row I/A return, albeit based upon the transposed row form on G♭. This rotation is less formally defined than rotation one, although most of the major thematic and harmonic ideas return—for instance: (1) the interaction between rows I/A and I/B from section one (mm. 177–184); (2) the interaction between rows I/C, I/D and I/E (mm. 185–197); and (3) the row I/C melody played by the first violins (mm. 198–204). Despite these similarities, however, an important difference, and one which provides a sense of structure to rotation two, is the uni-directional increase in rhythm and orchestral texture that lasts throughout the rotation. The immense rhythmic energy that ends part two (at m. 206) elides with part three, generating the climatic passage of the movement.

An abridged rotation three begins at m. 207 with two realizations of row I/A: the first statement is played by the divisi first violins in their highest possible register, followed by statements from the celli and double basses. To be noted, however, is that the harmonic form of row I/C has enlarged in scale to now encompass three instrumental groups. Section two begins at m. 226: here, harmonic presentations of rows I/C and I/D appear simultaneously throughout, once again segregated to different instruments. In the final section (beginning at m. 254), melodic realizations of row I/A appear with harmonic support by row I/C cast in unmeasured tremolos and at a triple *piano* dynamic level.

Movement Two

The second movement, marked *Allegro molto*, is a ternary form; each part is also a ternary design. The thematic idea dominating the opening thirty-three measures of the a section (from part A) contains two motives X and Y: motive X is a modified inversion of motive W; Figure 5.3 illustrates the two motives in their characteristic realizations.

The contrasting middle section lasts from mm. 34–63 and also features two prominent motives. The first, motive Y, contains two components: a B-A-C-H motive followed by an arpeggiated D Major triad; the second, i.e., motive Z, is a modified version of motive X that is inverted in contour. Motives W and X reappear in section a' (mm. 64–101), albeit with a greater amount of imitation between them than earlier.

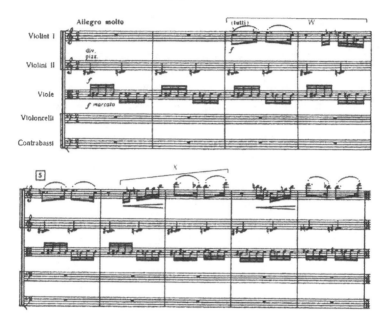

Figure 5.3 *Music for String Orchestra*, mov. 2, mm. 1–9

Part B of the movement begins at m. 102; it is also a ternary design. The outer sections feature a series of tertian-based homophonic chord progressions; a B-A-C-H motive functions as a bass line for the chord progressions.

As way of contrast, however, successive realizations of the B-A-C-H motive imitated at different intervals make up a large portion of the middle section (mm. 117–135); four-voice harmonies in unmeasured tremolos function as harmonic support during this portion of the design.

Part A' begins at m. 136; like part A, it is a ternary design. The first section retains the dialogue between motives W and X, as does the contrasting middle section's (mm. 160–187) interaction between its motives Y and Z. The interaction between motives W and X at m. 188 implies a return to the opening section. However, at m. 215 these motives are abandoned, signaling the beginning of the coda, one characterized by a dramatic increase in rhythmic activity from the lower supporting chromatic lines (there is a gradual shift from eighth notes to unmeasured tremolo figures) and the harmonic progressions from part B. The movement ends with an aggressive octave/unison statement of motive W played by all the strings.

Movement Three

The third movement, marked *Adagio religioso*, is a ternary form; parts A and A' are also cast in a ternary design and distinguished by chromatic motion by the celli and double basses and a violin melody that is constructed from row III/A (the two tone rows from the movement are illustrated in Figure 5.4).

Figure 5.4 Row forms of *Music for String Orchestra*, mov. 3

The ternary design of the outer parts is generated from two different types of chordal accompaniments: the outer sections (mm. 1–18 and 33–37) contain the three-chord progression shown in Figure 5.5; the middle section from mm. 19–32 is based upon another tertian-based progression cast in a characteristic eighth-note/sixteenth-note rhythm.

Row III/B dominates part B (mm. 38–71). The middle part contains five repetitions of this twelve-tone melody; with successive repetitions, the register and dynamic level increases. In addition, the supporting contrapuntal lines also increase in number with each repetition, to ultimately generate a five-voice texture that demarcates the climax of the movement.

Part A' begins at m. 71 and elides with the culminating moment of part B. The part contains three repetitions of row III/A; with each repetition, the melody decreases in register and dynamic level.

A short coda begins at m. 88 and contains two gestures: (1) the harmonic progression from mm. 19–32 (i.e., section b from part A); and (2) a statement of the series of harmonies from the outset of the movement (i.e., section a from part A). The movement ends calmly with an A Major triad.

Figure 5.5 *Music for String Orchestra*, mov. 3, mm. 1–24

Movement Four

Table 5.1 displays the various parts of the rondo-designed final movement, along with the corresponding measure numbers. The refrain, shown in Figure 5.6, is distinguished by a three-phrase melody. Aside from one instance (mm. 137–170), each refrain replicates this melody one octave lower, thereby forging the distinction between parts A and A'.

Table 5.1 Formal design of *Music for String Orchestra*, mov. 4

Measure no.:	1	14	26	55	65	78	92	106	137	170	184
Part:	A	A'	B	B'	A	A'	A''	C	A	B	B'

Measure no.:	194	218	229	247
Part:	C	A	A'	Coda

Figure 5.6 *Music for String Orchestra,* **mov. 4, mm. 1–15**

The first episode is characterized by a melody that contains numerous agogic rhythms which are separated by two sixteenth notes. Like the refrain, the two occurrences of this episode (mm. 26–54 and 170–183) are immediately repeated two octaves lower with slightly different accompanimental material. The second episode is essentially a three-voice chord progression that is repeated several times during its two occurrences (mm. 106–136 and 194–217).

The coda beginning at m. 247 contains two sections. The first includes several statements of the refrain theme, accompanied by motivic fragments of the same theme. The second section begins at m. 309. While some elements of the refrain theme remain, surprisingly, the three-chord progression that characterized much of the outer parts from movement three pervades the remainder of the movement, providing an interesting harmonic association between the composition's final two movements.

Sinfonia da camera

Kokkonen began work on his string orchestra *Sinfonia da camera* in the spring of 1961 immediately following the completion of the second symphony; it was finished in June of the next year. The four-movement chamber orchestra work (the piece is scored for four first violins, three second violins, two violas, two cellos and one double bass) was the result of a commission by the Lucerne Festival Strings and its long-time conductor Rudolf Baumgartner, who premiered the piece in Lucerne on 18 November 1962. The work was awarded the 1964 Finnish Broadcasting Company's Award for best orchestral composition.

The B-A-C-H motive features prominently throughout the work: the quote was meant as an act of homage to the composer Kokkonen admired above all others throughout his life. However, the motive was also intended as a tribute to the ensemble that commissioned the work: in 1960 Kokkonen heard a performance of Bach's *Art of the Fugue* by the Lucerne Strings and was deeply moved by the work as well as the level of musicianship of the ensemble.

Movement One

The two rows shown in Figure 5.7 dominate movement one, marked *Moderato*. Of particular importance is Row I/A: not only does the row contain the B-A-C-H motive as its first four order positions, but also a transposed and inverted form of the motive, as its last four order positions (i.e., D♯-E-C♯-D); the middle four order positions also form the chromatic B-A-C-H tetrachord, albeit reordered {F,F♯,G,G♯}. Only four row forms of row I/A are used: P_{10} (i.e., the row illustrated), P_6, RI_6, I_{11} and RI_3. Significantly, all four row forms contain the B-A-C-H motive or its retrograde, i.e., H-C-A-B, thereby generating a degree of harmonic association between the four rows.

Figure 5.7 Row forms of *Sinfonia da camera*, mov. 1

The movement is a tripartite design. In part one, mm. 1–22, the P_{10} row form is prominent. The B-A-C-H motive is presented in various realizations both melodically and harmonically, making it the most aurally identifiable feature—although it should be noted that the somewhat complex polyphony between instrumental groups realized with syncopated rhythms makes it at times difficult to perceive the motive. Figure 5.8 contains a representative passage from the opening four measures.

The design of part two (mm. 22–59) includes a long-range strategy of rhythmic diminution. Beginning at m. 22, there is a constant eighth-note rhythm that underlines the musical activity, which at m. 33 changes to a sixteenth-note; by m. 54, melodic lines in sixteenth-note rhythms are harmonically supported by unmeasured tremolos by the strings. Part two also contains two new features as regards pitch. First is the appearance of row I/B: corresponding with the increased rhythmic activity is an increased prominence of this row and its associated distinctive rhythm. A second feature of part two is the large number of transpositions of the B-A-C-H motive as a substitution for row I/A.

Part three begins at m. 60. The texture is quite complex as there are frequently four simultaneous layers of melodic activity; further, the rhythmic values of these various levels decrease significantly compared with part two. Although various forms of row I/A are realized in a *Klangfarben* manner among the different contrapuntal voices (P_6, P_{10} and I_3 are the most prevalent rows here), row I/B appears at the climax in mm. 72–76 by the first and second violins and in an augmented rhythm. The movement ends quietly with a verticalized twelve-tone sonority; the

ordering of the final four pitches suggests that the P_{10} row form of row I/A
serves as the harmonic source for the final measures.

Figure 5.8 *Sinfonia da camera*, mov. 1, mm. 1–4

Movement Two

Two rows serve as the basis for the second movement, marked *Allegro non
troppo* (the rows are illustrated in Figure 5.9). Row II/A is quite similar to
row I/A from movement one: there are six invariant order positions and
except for the G, the remaining pitches are only slightly reordered. The
reordering of the row introduces an ordered pattern of interval classes 1 and
3 between groups of three pitches (for example, A-C-B (3,1), F♯-F-A♭ (1,3)

and E♭-E-G (1,3) (D and C♯, order positions 10 and 11, and B♭, order position 1, generate a further (1,3) interval-class pattern)). The interval pattern proves to be the basis of virtually all the pitch material that is not directly procured from either row II/A or II/B. As means of illustration, Figure 5.10, from mm. 5–8, shows how a statement of P_1 (the initial portion of the row's realization is played by the cellos and double basses in mm. 5–6, the remainder by the violins 5, 6 and 7 in mm. 6–8) is supported by numerous passages of minor 3^{rds} (interval-class 3) and minor 2^{nds} (interval-class 2).

Figure 5.9 Row forms of *Sinfonia da camera*, mov. 2

The movement is a ternary form; both parts A and B are also a ternary design (part A' is abridged and leads to a coda). The movement opens energetically with numerous statements of row II/A; as just noted, such realizations of the row are supported by chains of minor 2nd and 3rd intervals. At m. 22, tension subsides and section b begins (mm. 22–37): the section contains realizations of row II/B in predominantly long rhythmic values; row II/A is absent. A return to the vigorous opening begins at m. 38: both rows II/A and II/B are used in this section (mm. 38–51) and are once again harmonically supported by chains of minor 3rd intervals.

The contrasting part B begins at m. 52. The outer sections are based upon canonic statements of row II/B played by the violas and cellos. In the middle section, however, the significance of the minor 3rd interval comes to the fore: any trace of rows II/A or II/B is absent; instead, each of the seven violins play a different minor 3rd, leading to the generation of the twelve-note harmony in m. 61.

The energetic opening from part A reappears at m. 78, signaling the end of part B. Part A' is complex and combines statements of both rows II/A and II/B with numerous chains of minor 3^{rds}. A coda begins at m. 102 and is nearly consumed by minor 3^{rds}. The movement ends calmly with a symmetrical chord that features both minor 2^{nds} and minor 3^{rds}.

Figure 5.10 *Sinfonia da camera*, mov. 2, mm. 4–10

Movement Three

The scherzo-like third movement, marked *Molto vivace*, is distinctive from the other movements by its pitch material that is entirely based upon only one row ordering, shown in Figure 5.11; although a few row forms are used, the most prevalent are P_3 (the row form illustrated) and I_3. Further, even though there is a chromatic tetrachord in the row, it is not the B-A-C-H motive, but, rather, a transposed version using the pitches D♭-C-E♭-D. (A further distinction of the third movement from the other movements is that the various realizations of this {D♭,C,E♭,D} tetrachordal motive are not readily apparent aurally.) One important feature of the two row forms P_3 and I_3 is that they are often permuted; the most common rotation begins with the pitch G.

Figure 5.11 Row form of *Sinfonia da camera*, mov. 3

The movement is a ternary form, preceded by a six-measure introduction. Although not defined with any sense of cadential closure, it is possible to partition the outer parts into three sections based on the row forms used (part A' begins at m. 56): section one contains imitative textures and P row forms only; section two contains successive unison/octave statements of a P row form followed by an I row form; and section three contains numerous imitative statements of both P and I row forms. Six- and seven-note chords realized as unmeasured tremolos function as a mediating gesture between the three sections. In general, parts A and A' are characterized by a melody and accompaniment texture; the melodies are generated from linear presentations of row forms, while the accompanimental patterns are forged by a row form distributed among two or three stringed instruments.

Although the two row forms P_3 and I_3 (and, in particular, the permutations that begins on G) and the melody/accompaniment texture appear in part B (mm. 32–55), the central portion of the movement differs from part A in several interesting ways. First, virtually all the melodies are played only by solo instruments instead of using doublings. Second, there is a distinct segregation between the P and I row forms in this homophonic texture: the P forms are reserved for the melody only; the I forms are used for the accompaniment. Third, much longer rhythmic values are utilized for the melodic portion of the texture.

Movement Four

Movement four, marked *Andante*, is a tripartite design. Except for a small portion of part three noted below, the pitch material is generated from the two rows shown in Figure 5.12. Row IV/A is very similar to row I/A from movement one, providing a valuable inter-movement harmonic association. The slight change in order positions between the pitches F and G, however, introduces a feature to movement four that was not present in the earlier rows—namely, that the row's three tetrachords do not have to be re-organized in order to generate transpositional relationships between each other. Specifically, the order positions of the present row are such that the

second tetrachord, i.e., F♯-F-A♭-G, is a T_8 transposition of the B-A-C-H
tetrachord (i.e., order positions 1–4), while the third tetrachord is a T_{11}
relationship with the first tetrachord (in movement one, the T_8 relationship
between B-A-C-H and F♯-G-A♭-F was not as aurally vivid).

Figure 5.12 Row forms of *Sinfonia da camera*, mov. 4

Row IV/B shares some interesting relationships with row IV/A. While
only the initial order position remains the same—B♭ is the first pitch of
both rows—the ordering of the pitches in row IV/B is quite similar to row
IV/A. The end result is that even though the interval-class 5 that initiates
row IV/B suggests harmonic dissimilarity from row IV/A, the consistency
between the rows, as regards the order of pitches, does provide aural
familiarity between them.

The opening part of the movement is largely based upon a
Klangfarben-styled realizations of row IV/A. Part two (mm. 15–34) begins
with the appearance of row IV/B played as a unison statement by violins 1–
4: it is the first time in the movement that a complete row statement is
realized without moving among instruments. While part two contains
numerous statements of row IV/B, a chordal accompaniment based upon a
repeating sixteenth-note rhythmic figure and derived from row IV/A
gradually competes with row IV/B; by m. 30, the accompanimental chords
completely dominate the musical landscape.

Part three begins at m. 35: following the three inexplicable statements
of movement three's row, the remainder of the movement contains melodic
realizations of row IV/B; the vast majority of these statements are
retrograde forms and are harmonically supported in the lower strings by the
three transpositions of the B-A-C-H motive from row IV/A. Following one
final statement of the B-A-C-H motive played by the violin 1 (at m. 65) the
movement ends calmly with a sustained harmony obtained from the first
eight order positions of row IV/A.

Opus Sonorum

Kokkonen considered *Opus Sonorum* his "anti-Darmstadt" work: during his tenure during the 1950s as music critic for the Finnish newspapers *Ilta Sanomat* and *Uusi Suomi*, Kokkonen became increasingly alarmed by what he perceived to be an all-consuming need for the percussion section to dominate a work's structure in many of the compositions he had heard at various Darmstadt festivals. To this end, then, the *Opus Sonorum* was consciously scored for a traditional-sized orchestra without the use of percussion; however, a piano was included to generate the tonal nuances that would otherwise have been given to the section.

The three-movement *Opus Sonorum* (the movements are played without pause), like *Sinfonia da camera* from two years earlier, contains an intricate system of dodecaphonic relationships in which each movement contains three different row orderings. Of interest, however, are the fascinating harmonic relationships that exist between these various row orderings, associations that will be commented upon shortly.

Opus Sonorum was written during the latter part of 1964. The piece was premiered at a centenary concert in honor of Sibelius on 16 February 1965; Paavo Berglund conducted the Finnish Radio Symphony Orchestra for the concert. Its success was immediately recognized, and the composition has since been performed in numerous venues both in Finland and abroad. The composer was awarded the Finnish Broadcasting Company Award in 1966 for the work.

Movement One

The pitch material of the first movement, marked *Moderato*, is entirely generated from the three twelve-tone row orderings shown in Figure 5.13 (no other row forms of each ordering are used except for those illustrated); row I/A is the most frequently employed.

Figure 5.13 Row forms of *Opus Sonorum*, mov. 1

The movement is a four-rotation design: rotation one lasts from mm. 1–15; rotation two, mm. 16–30; rotation three, mm. 31–52; and rotation four, mm. 52–68 (there is an elision between rotations three and four). A vital feature of the movement is three pitch motives that pervade the movement, providing a sense of unity between each rotation. However, since these motives are not specifically associated with a particular row, it is more valuable to refer to their generalized contour shapes, as opposed to specific pitches and intervals. Figure 5.14 illustrates the three four-note pitch motives that pervade the movement; the motives are labeled P-MOT/A, P-MOT/B and P-MOT/C. Two omnipresent rhythmic motives—R-MOT/A and R-MOT/B—are also included.[1]

Figure 5.14 Pitch and rhythmic motives in *Opus Sonorum*, mov. 1

Each rotation contains two sections. The first section consists of an extended three-element, sentence-like structured melody. In order to provide a sense of unity, each of the three elements is based upon one of the pitch and rhythmic motives described above. The register and dynamic level increase with each successive element, thereby generating a gradual *crescendo* to the overall melody. Figure 5.15 illustrates the sentence-structured melody and supporting harmonies in mm. 7–13 from rotation one: of note is the thrice succession of P-MOT/A and the associated use of R-MOT/A (twice) and R-MOT/B (used for the final statement of P-MOT/A in mm 11–12).

While the first section of a rotation is melodic in nature, the second is essentially harmonic: six- to eight-note sonorities are played by the brass and woodwind instruments in various combinations. Of note is the consistent elision between the two sections, although the position of the elision changes in each instance. Despite the variety of harmonies that appear in this section, a characteristic of section two is the pervasive use of the two primary rhythmic motives, thereby engendering a sense of concordance from rotation to rotation.

The large-scale strategy of the movement, then, is to maintain the general design of each successive two-section rotation while altering the specific pitches, orchestration of the three-phrased melody and harmonic sonorities from both sections. With each subsequent rotation, there is a gradual increase to the overall range, dynamic level and texture, ultimately forging an all-encompassing *crescendo* in the final measures of the movement.

Figure 5.15 *Opus Sonorum*, mov. 1, mm. 7–13

Movement Two

The pitch material of the second movement, marked *Adagio non troppo*, is generated from the three rows illustrated in Figure 5.16. Row II/A is identical to row I/A. Row II/B is a new row ordering: its initial two pitches suggest that it is an inversional relationship of row II/A; however, by the third pitch, we realize that a different harmonic resource is in place. (A comparison between these rows does demonstrate, though, similarity as regards order-position relationships.) Finally, row II/C is the retrograde inversion row form of row II/B that begins on B; of note are several order-position relationships shared between these two latter rows. As a final observation, the first order position of all three rows is the pitch-class "B," a feature that Kokkonen often exploits during imitative, contrapuntal passages to suggest a tonal focus.

The movement is a two-rotation form preceded with a short introduction; like the first movement, each rotation contains two sections. The duration of rotation one is from m. 74 until m. 95. The first section (mm. 74–80) contains a melodic statement of row II/B by the horns and viola, with numerous repeating harmonies by the woodwinds derived from row II/A.

The second section is more contrapuntally active: in essence, the woodwinds and strings engage a dialogue in which an orchestral family contains a series of imitative statements of either rows II/B or II/C. Importantly, however, this imitation is harmonically supported by a continuous series of four triads—specifically, B♭ Major, F♯ minor, C minor and E Major (combined, the four triads generate a complete chromatic aggregate).

As section two unfolds, the instruments increase in register and dynamic level. Not only is the highest register achieved at the end of the section, but it is also the singular moment when the woodwinds and strings coalesce into an octave/unison statement.

Rotation two begins at m. 96. While the first rotation contained only two melodic statements of row II/B, there are now three (one each by the horns, cellos and solo trombone), as well as a realization of row II/A by the bassoon. And while the harmonic accompaniment from the first rotation was generated from row II/A, in the second rotation it is forged from all three rows at different points of this section. Further, there are passages in which the series of B♭ Major, F♯ minor, C minor and E Major triads are simultaneously heard. An additional point of note as regards the harmonic accompaniment involves rhythm: where the harmonic activity was cast in a sixteenth-note rhythmic setting in the earlier section, in the present section it is in triplet-sixteenth notes. In short, the scope of section one has dramatically increased compared with its counterpart from rotation one.

Perhaps as a balance to the expanded first section, section two, beginning at m. 109, is shorter in duration compared with its complement from the first rotation; however, the amount of imitation increases. The ending of the section also differs when compared with the first rotation: in particular, the accompaniment is now cast in a sixteenth-note rhythm and the dynamic level reaches triple *forte*—the loudest dynamic thus far in the movement. In addition, the section ends with the four-triad harmonic progression, now stated by the entire orchestra, also at a triple *forte* dynamic level.

Figure 5.16 Row forms of *Opus Sonorum*, mov. 2

A short coda (mm. 119–123) brings the movement to a calm ending. The first gesture of the section is an abridged statement of row II/B played by a solo bassoon, and is followed by an imitative passage by the woodwinds of row II/A.

Movement Three

As with the other two movements, the movement utilizes three rows (illustrated in Figure 5.17): row III/A is very similar to rows I/A and II/A— only the final order positions are slightly rearranged; row III/B is a T_5 transposition of row III/A. Row III/C, however, is a new row ordering: of note is the close relationship the row shares with row III/B, as regards the first five order positions.   A further important harmonic resource stems from movement two—namely, the four-triad series B♭ Major, F♯ minor, C minor and E Major.

The movement, marked *Allegro non troppo*, is an arch-form design— formally, A-B-C-B'-A'.   The opening part A, mm. 124–149, is characterized by an imitative texture, in which the thematic material, based on rows III/A (primarily) and III/B (secondarily), is cast in a somewhat capricious rhythmic setting. Of note is the bassoon accompaniment that articulates the series of four triads: while the majority of the supporting materials for the various thematic statements are either vertical trichords or melodic fragments forged from row III/A, the triad series from the opening measures establishes an important link with the vital series of harmonies from the second movement.

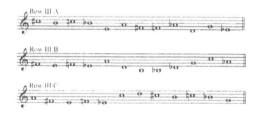

Figure 5.17 Row forms of *Opus Sonorum*, mov. 3

Part B lasts from m. 150 until m. 162. The section is distinguished by extensive use of the piano, where the right hand plays row III/C realized in scalar passages; the left hand, however, contains a series of dyads— specifically, D-B♭, C♯-F♯, C-G and B-C♯— suggesting the four triads that were introduced in the prior section. In effect, the scalar passages by the piano are harmonic support for the melodic realization of row III/A, played by the strings.

Part C begins at m. 163 and is almost entirely based upon row III/A. String ostinatos dominate the section—in fact, the one identifiable melody is a realization of row III/A by the violins in mm. 170–177, a passage that leads to the series of chords in mm. 175–181 that ends the section: (1) an E Major sonority by the brass; (2) C minor and F♯ minor combined by the woodwinds and the piano; (3) followed by a bitonal sonority comprised of B♭ and E Major triads, this time by the piano only.

Measures 182–201 incorporate most of the significant motives thus far; the fragmentary, almost improvisatory quality of the passage is suggestive of a brief development section. The section concludes with the same hexachord used to end the first section of part C, namely a combination of B♭ and E Major triads—however, now the sonority is played by the brass instruments and at a greater dynamic level.

The piano's scalar passagework is based upon row III/C and the string's melodic realization of row III/A returns at m. 202, demarcating part B' (it lasts from m. 202 until m. 210). New to the present part, however, is the addition of the complete B♭ Major, F♯ minor, C minor and E Major triads, also played by the strings.

At m. 211 row III/A is played by the violins in the rhythmic profile from the opening of the movement, identifying part A'. A coda, marked *Quasi ritenente*, begins at m. 237. It contains two opposing rhythmic processes. On one hand, there are several statements of row III/A, played by all the strings and woodwinds at the octave/unison, but realized in ever increasing rhythmic values. As contrast, however, the brass presents simultaneous realizations of row III/A and the series of four triads in a quasi-imitative fashion of eighth-note rhythms. It is only in the final measures that the brass becomes rhythmically aligned; the point coincides with the exhilarating ending containing a sustained bitonal chord of E and B♭, played by the entire orchestra at a triple *forte* dynamic level.

Symphonic Sketches

The *Symphonic Sketches* dates from 1968 and was written immediately following the third symphony as a commission from the Helsinki Festival. Kokkonen avoided labeling the work a symphony and instead preferred to add the more detached title of "sketch." The title is appropriate: while the composition contains many features in common with his four symphonies, the brevity of the movements—in particular, the second—and the circumscribed amount of motivic development throughout engender a quality of incompleteness, or, if you will, sketch, to the work.

The three-movement work was premiered on 16 May 1968; Paavo Berglund conducted the Finnish Radio Symphony Orchestra for the performance.

Movement One

The pitch material of the first movement, marked *Lamento*, is primarily based upon the three rows (and two row orderings) shown in Figure 5.18. Row I/B is the inversional form of row I/A that begins on D♭: the choice of these particular prime and inversional row forms ensures that the pitch classes B♭/A, D/E♭ and D♭/C/B remain as contiguous elements, forging a certain degree of harmonic invariance.

The movement is a bipartite design. Part one is distinguished by a pervasive ostinato that provides the harmonic support for various melodic gestures. The ostinato begins in m. 1 with the continuous repetition of the pitch C in a quarter-note rhythm by the tympani, harp, cellos and double basses At m. 20, however, the single pitch expands into a four-element eighth-note figure, <C4-D♭3-F3-E2>, which pervades until the end of part one (m. 30). The majority of the melodic material is stated by the first and second violins, although the horns play an important counter melody in mm. 15–30; numerous woodwind flourishes embellish the string melodies. Rows I/A and I/B feature prominently in these woodwind gestures.

Figure 5.18 Row forms of *Symphonic Sketches*, mov. 1

A brief interlude from mm. 31–32 contains interplay of fragments from both rows I/A and I/B between the woodwinds. Part two of the movement begins at m. 38: unlike part one, where the melodic material is primarily presented by the strings, an important amount of the melodic material in part two is also offered by the woodwinds. Further, row I/C plays a significant role in virtually every melodic gesture from part two until the culminating moment of the movement at m. 67. This is not to say that rows I/A and I/B are not used, only that their role is reserved as supportive material for these melodies. A further distinguishing feature between parts one and two is the greater melodic range of the various melodies and enlarged dynamic level in part two.

Following the climatic triple *forte* E Major triad in m. 67 (played by the entire orchestra), the dynamic level immediately diminishes to triple *piano*, where it remains throughout the short coda. There are two noteworthy features of the coda. First is the realization of movement two's row II/C in mm. 77–81 (the arpeggiated unfolding of this row takes place over a sustained E Major triad). A second feature is the inversional chromatic scales by the unmeasured string tremolos in mm. 82–85. The chromatic motion is significant, for it anticipates a similar procedure in the introduction of movement three.

Movement Two

The second movement, marked *Pezzo giocoso*, is a ternary form. The majority of the pitch material is generated from the twelve-tone rows illustrated in Figure 5.19. As a general rule, rows II/A and II/B are reserved for the melodic material of the movement and row II/C for the harmonic accompaniment. Row II/C can be partitioned into three successive tertian triads, followed by a fourth {C#,D#,F#} trichord; intervals of major or minor 3^{rds} separate the first triad from the second and the second triad from the third. While it is more common to find this "triad

row" partitioned to exploit its harmonic potential, it is occasionally realized
as a linear statement during the transitional passages between parts A and B
and between parts B and A'.

Figure 5.19 Row forms of *Symphonic Sketches*, mov. 2

The A and A' parts of the ternary form are associated by a similar
design, as regards orchestral texture: in both instances, lively interplay of
motivic elements from both the prime and inverted form of row II/A are
imitated between the woodwind instruments; a common rhythmic figure
associated with these motives is two sixteenth notes followed by an eighth.
The strings employ row II/B to a large extent, realized exclusively in eighth
notes. Measure 18 (matched by m. 101 in part A') represents the second
stage of the movement: the horns begin to state triads derived from row
II/C and support melodic material from rows II/A and II/B realized by the
violins. By m. 25 (m. 95 in the A' section) the rhythm of the violins'
melodic material has diminished to a constant sixteenth-note value.
Ultimately, by the end of parts A and A' all the violins, violas, woodwinds
and percussion state rows II/A and II/B; the cellos and contrabasses unfold
row II/B, partitioned into triads by the brass instruments. Despite the
matching increase in texture, rhythmic activity and harmonic complexity
between parts A and A', the two endings differ significantly: while a
marked decrease in these musical parameters begins at m. 49, leading to the
contrasting part B, in part A' there is a relentless buildup of energy that
culminates with the triple *forte* E Major triads in m. 116 that conclude the
movement.

A transition constructed from melodic statements of row II/B
establishes part B (this portion of the movement begins in m. 60); virtually
all the pitch material of the short middle section is also obtained from this
row. Like the outer portions, the woodwinds contain important motivic
interplay, while the harmonically supportive strings respond with slightly
longer rhythmic values. Of note is the complete absence of the brass.

Movement Three

The majority of the pitch material of movement three, marked *Religioso*, is based upon the three row orderings shown in Figure 5.20: Row III/A is a twelve-tone row; rows III/B and III/C are both eight-note rows and inversionally related to each other. Given the extensive use of dodecaphonic procedures in the movement, it is somewhat surprising that the ten-measure introduction is devoid of twelve-tone writing. Rather, the introduction is based upon two inversional chromatic scales whose focal points are D and A♭. However, the chromatic lines not only utilize different instruments, but also divergent registers (in other words, successive elements of the *Klangfarben* inversional relationship are pitch-class related and not pitch related).

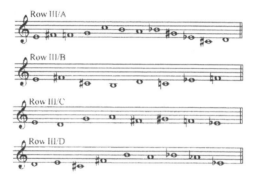

Figure 5.20 Row forms of *Symphonic Sketches*, mov. 3

The ternary-form movement proper commences in m. 11. Part one contains two sections: the first section is distinguished by various imitative realizations of row III/A played by the strings and cast in long, legato lines of a limited melodic range. In section two (mm. 25–35), the strings play unmeasured trills using pitch material derived from row III/A. The woodwinds and vibraphone generate an increase in orchestral texture by gradually superimposing motivic events above the string trills (derived from rows III/B (primarily) and III/C (occasionally)), realized in thirty-second or unmeasured tremolo note values.

The contrasting part B begins at m. 35: sustained pitches by the woodwinds and brass generate a hexachord whose pitches are registrally arranged to articulate E♭ Major and A/Dominant 7th ({A,C♯,E,G}) chords, and support harmonically melodic realizations of rows III/B and III/C played by the strings.

Figure 5.21 *Symphonic Sketches*, mov. 3, mm. 69–76

Part A' begins at m. 43 with a series of unmeasured string tremolos unfolding successive realizations of rows III/C and III/D. The passage concludes at m. 55 with a cadential gesture generated from a five-measure brass chorale. A second brass chorale begins at m. 65; however, the cadential gesture is extended by the increase in textural density through the addition of the woodwinds, and leads to the climax of the movement at m.

75 (mm. 69–76 are illustrated in Figure 5.21). This luminous moment, however, is short lived: by m. 78 the dynamic level has dropped from triple *forte* to *pianissimo*, contributing to the calm ending in which a quarter-note ostinato reiterates an E Major triad.

Cello Concerto

Kokkonen's Cello Concerto, his only work for solo instrument and orchestra, was written in 1969 immediately following the *Symphonic Sketches*. Its reception has been remarkable, and it is by far the most performed Finnish cello concerto of all time. The work is in five movements, although the last three (i.e., the *Adagio* third, the cadenza fourth and the *Vivace* fifth) are to be played without pause. It is dedicated to the famous Finnish architect Alvar Aalto. Although Kokkonen had long admired Aalto's work, the two artists became close friends beginning in 1968 when Aalto designed the home in Järvenpää in which Kokkonen and his family lived. Regarding the concerto, Kokkonen stated that:

> Three people were immediately involved in the composition of this piece. It is dedicated to the architect Alvar Aalto, for this was the first major work which I completed in our new house, which Aalto designed. The dedication is not merely an expression of thanks and admiration for this great architectural master, however: when composing this concerto I often remembered my extensive conversations with Alvar Aalto, which made me aware more than ever before of the close relationship between music and architecture—a relationship much deeper and richer than words can express. The piece is written for Arto Noras. In the summer of 1966 I had the opportunity to hear his first-rate playing in the Tchaikovsky Competition. Then, in Moscow, we agreed that I should write a cello concerto for him. The third person whom I should like to mention here is my mother, who died in June 1969. The song-like theme in the *Adagio* third movement is thematically very close to the little organ piece I wrote in her memory. It is not a dirge, however, but the expression of light-filled memory overshadowed by longing.

The highlight of the work is unquestionably the slow middle movement described by Kokkonen: its hauntingly beautiful melody is one of the most profound from Kokkonen's oeuvre. As Kokkonen notes in the quote above, the music is closely related to the organ piece dating from 1969 entitled *Surusoitto* (*Funeral Music*).

The Cello Concerto received its premiere in Helsinki on 16 October 1969: the soloist was Arto Noras; Jorma Panula conducted the Helsinki Philharmonic Orchestra.

Movement One

The movement begins with a three-note motive harmonized with perfect 4^{ths} and 5^{ths} intervals (see Figure 5.22). The motive represents a motto that demarcates the beginning and end points of each section. Virtually all the pitch material in the movement is derived from the three rows shown in Figure 5.23. Row I/B is particularly interesting, for there are two possible options for order positions 8 and 9, thereby suggesting two cadential gestures. Row I/C is an inversional row form of row I/B.

Figure 5.22 Recurring motive in Cello Concerto, mov. 1

Figure 5.23 Row forms of Cello Concerto, mov. 1

The movement is a tri-partite design, followed by a cadenza and final cadential gesture; both parts one and two contain two sections. While the two parts are differentiated by divergent tempi—*Moderato mosso* for part one and *Allegro* for part two—each contain similar bipartite designs: section one from both parts (mm. 1–25 for part one; mm. 52–93 for part two) utilizes primarily row I/A, while section two (mm. 26–51 for part one; mm. 94–141 for part two) largely employs row I/B.

A significant decrease in tempo (the marking is *Poco più lento*) and texture occurs at m. 144, demarcating part three; the changes introduce a more relaxed mood into the music. Associated with part three is an alteration in pitch material: except for the cadential gesture that announces the cadenza (the gesture uses row I/B), it is virtually all obtained from row I/C. Part three contains three sections: section one (mm. 144–161) is arranged as a dialogue between the soloist and strings; in section two (mm. 162–171) the texture changes from a musical dialogue to one where the soloist is accompanied by triadic harmonies realized in an eighth-note rhythm by both the strings and woodwinds. The soloist is absent in section three (mm. 172–182), in which an orchestral tutti passage announces the cadenza beginning at m. 183.

The cadenza utilizes all three rows: it opens with row I/A, is followed by extensive use of row I/B, while row I/C appears just after the midpoint; it ends with row I/A and ultimately, a chromatic scale harmonized with sixths. The scale segues to the final rousing orchestral tutti, bringing the movement to a thrilling close on B♭ Major.

Movement Two

Figure 5.24 contains the three twelve-note rows that generate a significant percentage of the pitch material from the ternary-designed second movement, marked *Allegretto*. There are interesting features about these rows worthy of comment. First is the numerous inter-movement harmonic relationships generated from the close relationship shared between the order positions of the primary row of the movement, row II/A, and row I/C from movement one. A second association is between rows II/A and II/C: although they are different row orderings, the first half of row II/A contains the same pitch-class content as the latter half of row II/C (and vice versa). A third correlation is the T_5 relationship between order positions 2 to 6 and 7 to 11 in Row II/B and the T_6 connection between each half of row II/C. These transpositional associations are not just interesting mathematical features of each row—rather, Kokkonen often phrases musical passages to specifically highlight these associations. A final harmonic relationship is the invariant pitches shared between the final four pitches of row II/A and first four pitches of row II/C. The invariant pitches provide a link between these rows, thereby generating melodies of more extensive dimension.

The movement opens with a four-measure introduction set in a ⅝ meter that establishes its pervasive buoyant and charming mood. Part A of the ternary form is generated from two asymmetrical phrases: the first, ranging from mm. 5–8 is, like the woodwind, harp and string accompaniment, completely derived from row II/A. The second, more lengthy phrase is from mm. 9–25: it begins an octave higher than phrase one and is expanded through the numerous repetitions of fragments from rows II/B and II/C, mostly cast in a triplet-sixteenth rhythm (although row II/A is still the primary row for the pitch material of the accompaniment).

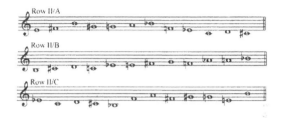

Figure 5.24 Row forms of Cello Concerto, mov. 2

Some distinguishing features of the contrasting part B (mm. 26–37) include: (1) the extensive duration of a $\frac{6}{8}$ meter; (2) the emphasis of sustained C Major triads played by the low woodwinds, harp and cellos; (3) the exhaustive use of row II/A (the sole exception is the realization of row II/C played by the soloist in m. 34); and (4) a much thinner orchestral texture, when compared with part A.

The motivic ideas from the opening recur at m. 38, demarcating part A'. An increase in rhythmic activity is immediately apparent, as every eighth note is now subdivided with three triplet-sixteenth notes. Although there is liberal use of all three rows in the section, row I/A is by far the most prevalent. Part A' resembles an arch design, as regards texture: at m. 38 the soloist is accompanied by strings; m. 46, the woodwinds are added. The central portion of the section begins at m. 67 and is scored for the entire orchestra, but without soloist. At m. 74, the dialogue between soloist and orchestra returns; however, the brass is now added. The movement ends with a single flute, tympani and harp all quietly playing repetitions of the pitch E.

Movement Three

The core of the concerto is the ternary-designed third movement. Two rows are the source for much of the pitch material in the movement (the rows appear in Figure 5.25). An important feature of the fourteen-pitch row III/A (the pitches C and G are duplicated) is its associated tonal harmonic progression, shown in Figure 5.26. The threat of aural fatigue from the consistent association between row III/A and its supporting harmonic progression is averted by the gradual registral ascent of row A and the deliberate increase in orchestral density with each row repetition.

Despite the invariance between the first two pitches of row III/B and row III/A, its greater length (twenty-two pitches) and divergent harmonic support from that of row III/A (different tertian harmonies sustain row III/B, while in the central section of the work, mm. 39–48, non-tertian harmonies are used) suggest a different formal role between the two rows.

Figure 5.25 Row forms of Cello Concerto, mov. 3

Figure 5.26 Recurring progression in Cello Concerto, mov. 3

Table 5.2 illustrates the design of the movement, one generated from the use of rows III/A and III/B; of note is that the outer parts are also a ternary design. Contrast in harmonic material, however, is not the sole criterion for the ternary form. For instance, while it was noted that part B is largely based on row III/B (and its particular harmonic support), this divergent pitch material also correlates with the soloist's rather improvisatory-styled lines, lending a cadenza-like quality to this portion of the movement.

Movement Four

The fourth movement is a solo cadenza: although it utilizes all the primary rows from the previous three movements, a significant percentage is based upon movement three's row III/A. The movement's design is shown in Table 5.3.

Table 5.2 Formal design of Cello Concerto, mov. 3

Introduction

Measure no.	Description of formal unit
1–7/b.2	(Utilizes row III/A.)

Part A

Measure no.	Description of formal unit
7/b.3–19	Section a (utilizes row III/A).
20–25	Section b (utilizes row III/B).
26–38	Section a' (utilizes row III/A).

Part B

Measure no.	Description of formal unit
39–48	Cadenza-like sections that utilize both rows III/A and III/B with harmonies not found in parts A and A'.

Part A'

Measure no.	Description of formal unit
49–57	Section a (utilizes row III/A).
58–62	Section b (utilizes row III/B).
63–71	Section a' (utilizes row III/A).

Coda[2]

Measure no.	Description of formal unit
72–77	Utilizes fragments of row A.

Table 5.3 Formal design of Cello Concerto, mov. 4

Rehearsal no.	Description of solo material
(opening)	Two statements of Movement three, row A harmonized with a similar progression to Figure 5.26.
A	Movement three, row III/A; melody contains trills.
B	• Movement two, row II/B; thirty-second note scale. • Movement three, row IIIA; melody contains trills. • Movement two, row II/B; triplet-sixteenth scale. • Movement two, row II/A.
C	Movement three, row IIIA; expressed as harmonics.

D	• Movement two, row IIA; original rhythm with an ending in harmonics. • Movement two, row II/C; a descending two-octave scale in sixteenth notes.
E	• Movement two, row II/B; an ascending two-octave scale in triplet-sixteenth notes. • Movement one, row I/A; eighth and sixteenth notes.
F	Movement three, row III/A; two complete statements of this row supported by arpeggiated chords.

Movement Five

Cast as a ternary form, the pitch material of the brief final movement, marked *Allegro vivace*, is largely generated from the three rows shown in Figure 5.27.

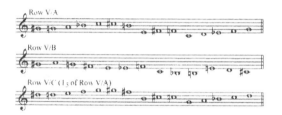

Figure 5.27 Row forms of Cello Concerto, mov. 5

A distinctive feature of the movement is a pervasive rhythmic motive comprised of two sixteenth notes followed by an eighth. Part B (mm. 55–81) is distinguished from the outer parts by the extensive use of row III/A from movement three, realized in long rhythmic values (although the extensive sixteenth-note accompaniment preserves the rhythmic energy from parts A and A').   Further, the row now appears without the characteristic triadic harmonization that was such a vital part of its realization in the third and fourth movements. A lively coda begins at m. 116; until the appearance of a B♭ Major triad in the penultimate measure, E Major—played as both sonorities and scalar figures—pervades the final section.

Inauguratio

Inauguratio dates from 1971, the same year as Kokkonen's fourth symphony. The work was commissioned by the Helsinki Festival and was intended to be performed at the inaugural ceremony of Helsinki's Finlandia Hall, the city's largest concert hall; the title is a direct reference to its utilitarian role for the ceremony. However, extended delays on the Hall's construction ultimately prevented its completion at the appointed time. Instead, the composition's premiere took place during the summer Helsinki Festival on 5 September 1971; Jorma Panula conducted the Helsinki Philharmonic at Helsinki's House of Culture for the performance.

Although it is certainly not as well known as Kokkonen's symphonies or orchestral works such as *Sinfonia da Camera* or *Opus Sonorum*, *Inauguratio* does provide a valuable introduction to the composer's compositional style on at least three counts. First, the work contains a number of different twelve-tone rows, but integrates them with tertian-based sonorities—an aspect, to varying degrees, in many of Kokkonen's twelve-tone compositions. Second, *Inauguratio* features his compositional practice of using small motivic cells as the basis from which the composer gradually develops larger and more complex melodies and harmonic structures. Third, the brevity of *Inauguratio*—performances of the work are typically around eight minutes in duration—makes the composition of manageable length to easily comprehend its salient features.

The opening twenty-four measures are an introduction. The work begins with two inversionally-related motives that emanate from A4; tonal centricity upon the pitch is generated by unmeasured tremolos and pizzicatos from the strings. The idea of a single pitch—and specifically, the concert pitch from which an orchestra would organize itself at the beginning a work—suggests an association with the title, i.e., an inauguration of something new (in this case, a new building). The two motives quickly superimpose, with several of the woodwinds and the three trumpets realizing them in different rhythmic patterns ranging from eighth-, triplet eighth-, sixteenth- and quintuplet sixteenth-notes. A vertical sonority in m. 14 derived from the pitches of the two motives stops the process and a new, six-note motive emanating from D4 appears; the motive is an exact transposition of the opening motive that moved upwards from A. As before, the motive is represented in different rhythmic values and presented in a gradual *crescendo*, as regards dynamic level and orchestral texture, culminating with the vertical sonority in m. 24.

The five rows in Figure 5.28 represent the primary pitch resources for the remainder of *Inauguratio*. Row II is a rotated version of row I that begins on A♭. Row III is a different type of permutation upon row I: the first five order positions of row III are the last five order positions of row I, and the last five order positions of row III are the first five order positions of row I. Aside from the initial A♭-G pitches, rows IV and V share few relationships, as regards order positions. It should be noted, though, that the latter two rows are virtually always used to extend a melodic line initiated by one of the first three rows.

In section two (mm. 25–52) the texture becomes more contrapuntal. Rows I, II, IV and V are all extensively used and nearly always in a *Klangfarben* fashion.

The character of the music changes at m. 53 (the first measure of section three): row III becomes of paramount significance, with harmonic support from repetitions of the first portions of rows I and V and the chromatic motive {A,B♭,C,C♯,B}. The section ends at mm. 72–77 with the bitonal chord of C Major (played by the horns) and E♭ Major (played by the trombones), followed by six repetitions of an octave-unison statement of the pitch A.

Row III appears twice in section four—at m. 80 and m. 95; the majority of the melodic material, though, is generated from row I, often played by the violins in their high register, thus gradually engendering more prominence to the row. Section four is characterized by a series of seven harmonic dyads generated from row I and a repeating baseline of <F♯-C♯-E-A-B♭>; the two features form harmonic support for the various melodic gestures. Figure 5.29 illustrates the harmonic series' first appearance at m. 84.

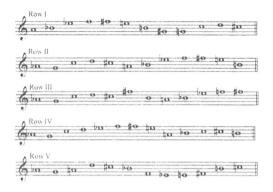

Figure 5.28 Row forms of *Inauguratio*

Figure 5.29 *Inauguratio*, mm. 83–89

The final section of *Inauguratio* begins at m. 129. An additional pitch is now added to each member of the harmonic dyad series, generating a series of tertian-based triads. Essentially, the ending is one large *crescendo*, as regards orchestral texture and dynamic level. The section begins with statements of rows II and III played by the violins and interpolated with the series of triads. After m. 150, though, the rows are eliminated and the ending consists solely of repetitions of the triad series among the orchestral families, bringing the work to a thrilling conclusion with an A Major triad played by the entire orchestra at a triple *forte* dynamic level.

...durch einen Spiegel...

This interesting composition dates from 1976, the same year as Cello Sonata and the String Quartet No. 3. It is scored for four first violins, three second violins, two violas, two cellos, one double bass and harpsichord; the complement of strings is identical to *Sinfonia da camera* from fifteen years earlier. The connection with *Sinfonia* extends further: the work was commissioned by the Lucerne Festival Strings and is dedicated to Rudolf Baumgartner. Both Baumgartner and his ensemble premiered the four-movement work (the second, third and fourth movements are to be played without pause) on 25 August 1977 as part of the concert commemorating the conductor's sixtieth birthday.

Movement One

The first movement, marked *Andante*, is cast in a ternary form; part one is also a ternary design. The movement opens with a seven-note sonority: the chord combines D and E♭ Major triads with the pitch E (the sonority's first appearance is shown in Figure 5.30). The "bitonal" sonority is an important feature of the movement: it appears numerous times as an independent sonority, where it functions as a type of motto. However its more important role is to provide harmonic support for the three major thematic ideas of the movement.

The rows generating these three themes are shown in Figure 5.31: rows I/B and I/C are the retrograde and inverted forms, respectively, of row I/A (note that the D/E♭ bitonal chord is derived from the latter order positions of row I/A). Interestingly, the contours of these rows remain virtually unchanged throughout the movement.

Figure 5.30 Bitonal chord from the opening of ...*durch einen Spiegel*...

Figure 5.31 Row forms of ...*durch einen Spiegel*..., mov. 1

The opening "a" section of part A (mm. 1–16) is comprised of the D/E♭ bitonal chord played by the harpsichord and the seven violins in their high register supporting a unison statement of row I/A played by the five remaining strings. A contrasting "b" section begins at m. 17. Here, the violins play various transpositions of the D-E♭ bitonal chord, supporting a statement of row I/B played by the lower strings. The return of row I/A at m. 40 demarcates section a', played now by the cellos only; however, several transpositions of the bitonal sonority support the various realizations of row I/B, as opposed to the single transposition level of the D/E♭ sonority from the opening.

Part B begins at m. 47. Instead of the melody and accompaniment that characterized part A, the texture becomes more imitative, using motivic fragments derived from row I/A. Of note is the importance of row I/C (the row's first appearance is at m. 60).

A transitional passage from mm. 80–86 leads to part A'. Its primary divergence from part A is the bitonal sonority supporting statements of row I/A: in part A the seven-note harmony is sustained, while in the latter part it is presented imitatively by the seven violins; the remaining strings play octave/unison statements of row I/A. The movement ends calmly with a quadruple *piano* dynamic at m. 106, where a final presentation of the sustained D/E♭ bitonal harmony supports the harpsichord's E Major triads. Movement two begins without pause.

Movement Two

The scherzo-like second movement, marked *Allegro* (the metronome marking is ♩ = 132) is, like the first, a ternary form. The vast majority of the pitch material is derived from row I/A.

Three prominent motives are established in the opening twenty-measure introduction (these are illustrated in Figure 5.32). Motive B is a series of alternating interval-5 cycles; motives A and C are retrogrades of each other and derived from row I/A. One frequent procedure is to generate octatonic scalar passages by sequentially transposing the {B♭,A,F♯,E} tetrachord. For instance, in mm. 113–115 a series of transpositions of the tetrachord articulate the pitches B♭-A♭-G-F-E-D-C♯, i.e., the octatonic collection $OCT_{1,2}$; the passage is immediately reinforced by a series of eight-voiced octatonic sonorities played by the harpsichord in mm. 116.

Motive A   Motive B   Motive C

Figure 5.32 Three motives in *...durch einen Spiegel...*, **mov. 2**

Part A begins at m. 126: the overall strategy is to unfold successive realizations of row I/B, which over the course of Part A generates a two-octave ascent in register by the violins and increase in dynamic level from *pianissimo* to *fortissimo*.

Part B begins at m. 161. Measured tremolo figures support two statements of a T_5 transposed version of row I/A (at m. 168 and 183). The extended rhythmic values that realize these themes contrast with the rhythmically active supporting harmonies.

A transition, based upon motives A, B and C, begins at m. 192. Part A' begins at m. 200: the melodic material is dominated by the same thematic ideas and rhythmic motives generated from row I/B that characterized part A. For instance, the theme gradually ascends in register and increases in dynamic level through numerous repetitions of row segments. At m. 220 (the culminating point of the ascent), rows I/A, I/B and I/C are each stated in octave/unison by the violas, cellos and double bass in long rhythmic values and at a triple *forte* dynamic level. In the short transition to movement three (mm. 243–248) statements of row I/A and its retrograde row form are realized at a *piano* dynamic level by the solo double bass, viola and cello in a triplet eighth-note rhythm that, when combined with the *rallentando* tempo indication, anticipate the tempo and metric setting of the next movement.

Movement Three

The ternary-form third movement, marked *Allegro ma non troppo*, is distinguished from the earlier two movements by a new row ordering. In total, three rows are employed (the rows are illustrated in Figure 5.33): (1) although row III/A (identical to row I/A) is rarely stated in its entirety, four- to eight-note segments of it are frequently used; (2) row III/B, a retrograde row form of row III/A beginning on E with the interpolated pitches E♭, D, F and E; and (3) row III/C, a row ordering related to row III/B.

Part A of the ternary form contains interplay between rows III/B and III/C by the violins. At m. 261, however, the dialogue is abandoned and we hear segments from each of the three rows; importantly, the violin register increases with each successive row statement. Further, these row statements are harmonically supported by linear presentations of an $OCT_{0,1}$ octatonic collection by the lower strings, and cast in sixteenth-note rhythms.

Figure 5.33 Row forms of ...*durch einen Spiegel...*, mov. 3

Part B begins at m. 296. An ostinato based on the {Eb,D,F,E} tetrachord is played by the violas and cellos and supports three melodic phrases played by the pizzicato violins: the first contains the latter portion of row III/C; the second and third are statements of row III/B.

Part A' begins at m. 318. Melodic realizations of the latter portion of row III/B and the first half of row III/C are played by the violins in their highest register. However, unlike part A, a sixteenth-note rhythmic pattern sustains these melodic statements from the outset of part A'. Further, instead of octatonic collections generating this supporting material, continuous repetitions of fragments from row III/B are now used. The movement ends with a sustained A Major triad played at a triple *forte* dynamic level.

A brief transition to the final movement (mm. 338–343) recalls Part B's material: three measures of the four-note ostinato {Eb,D,F,E} played by the lower strings is followed by a fragment of row III/A, played by pizzicato violins. The tempo of the transition is markedly slower than the third movement, and prepares the listener for the *Adagio* final movement.

Movement Four

The pitch material of the final movement is entirely generated from the three rows shown in Figure 5.34. Row IV/A is a new row ordering; rows IV/B and IV/C are identical to rows III/B and I/A, respectively, and are used to engender a recapitulative quality to the final movement.

The movement opens with an arpeggiated bitonal chord played by the harpsichord. However, while bitonal chords were separated by a semitone in the first movement (for instance, a hexachord generated from combining D Major and Eb Major triads), the chord is now forged from two triads a Major 2nd apart—in m. 344, for instance, by combining C Major and D Major together.

Figure 5.34 Row forms of *...durch einen Spiegel...*, mov. 4

The movement is essentially structured as a series of different imitative passages; with each passage there is an overall increase in dynamic level and orchestral density. The design of the movement is illustrated in Table 5.4.

Table 5.4 Formal Design of *...durch einen Spiegel...*, mov. 4

Measure no.	Description of formal unit
344	Imitative statements of row IV/A realized between a solo violin and viola.
349	Imitative statements of row IV/A realized between solo viola and cello. Harmonic support is a C/D Major bitonal chord.
353	One statement of IV/A: first portion is played by the solo viola and cello in unison; latter half by double bass in harmonics. Seven violins play bitonal harmony D/E Major.
357	Several imitative statements of row IV/A are shared among all the stringed instruments (playing unmeasured tremolos at a dynamic level of *pianissimo*).
364	Imitative statements of row III/C played by the violins (the first appearance of the row in the movement).
366	Fragments of row IV/C support a unison statement of row IV/A by the violas and cellos played at a *mezzo-forte* dynamic level.
370	Unison statement of row I/A begins at *fortissimo* and decreases to triple *piano* by m. 374.

At m. 375 the harpsichord plays a C/D♭ Major bitonal chord. The change in harmony demarcates a coda; however, it also recalls the opening of the work itself—and especially with the numerous statements of row I/A that consume the ending and the return of the opening tempo (♩ = 66–72). For instance, at m. 381 there is an octave/unison statement of row I/A played by all the strings at a triple *forte* dynamic level (the harpsichord even plays a version of the row harmonized with triads). The final measures of the work contain one last instance of row I/A, now played *arco* at a *pianissimo* dynamic level by the violas, cellos and double bass, followed by a sustained harmony comprised of C, D and E Major triads played by the violins and violas; the cellos and double bass complete the harmony with three repetitions of a unison pitch E played *pizzicato*.

Il paesaggio

Il paesaggio was commissioned by the city of Järvenpää for the inaugural ceremony that opened the Järvenpää Concert Hall on 13 February 1987. The work was premiered by the Järvenpää Chamber Orchestra, conducted by Jukka-Pekka Saraste. The Italian title translates as "landscape": as a composer who obsessively eschewed extra-musical associations in his music, Kokkonen was careful to point out that the title referred to the landscape around Lake Tuusula, and should only be thought of as the starting point for the composition and not a musical depiction of the landscape itself.

Il paesaggio is scored for a chamber orchestra—strings and a wind quintet. The work represents Kokkonen's final completed composition of consequence: his output had come to a near halt following the 1981 *Requiem*, and aside from two relatively short choral pieces, the only other composition of substance is the 1982 *Improvvisazione* for violin and piano.

The work is a two-rotation design with a coda (part two begins at m. 49); tempo may be used to separate each rotation into two associated sections. The first section of both rotations is relatively slow, with melodic lines of comparatively long rhythmic values used to realize the various rows used. Although the second section contains an increase in rhythmic activity over the first, there is also an increase in tempo in rotation two: section two in rotation one begins at m. 24 with the oboe flourish and unmeasured string tremolos; however, in rotation two, section two begins at m. 86 with the change in tempo from ♩ = 66 to ♩. = 72.

A coda begins at m. 124. The opening somber mood returns: the strings play an octave/unison realization of the primary row in long rhythmic values (the rows are discussed in the following paragraph); the row statement is harmonically supported by sustained octaves of the pitches A, G, and C (by the woodwinds). An interesting change, however, occurs at m. 139—the point in the score is marked "Enigma." The last eleven measures of the work contain "musical signatures" of three famous Finnish composers who, like Kokkonen, also lived in Järvenpää: at m. 139 is the octave/unison statement by the entire orchestra of the motive E-A-E♭-B-B♭-E-E♭ (for Jean Sibelius); in mm. 142–144 the oboe plays the motive E-B♭-E-G-A for (Erik Bergman); and in mm. 144–145 the flute plays the motive A-A-B-E-E for (Paavo Heininen).

The pitch material of *Il paesaggio* is based upon the P_6 row form of the ordering shown in Figure 5.35. Although P_6 is by far the most prominent row form in the work, the other rows of importance are illustrated in the same example.

Figure 5.35 Row forms of *Il paesaggio*

1. The row forms I_6, i.e., the inverted form of P_6, and (occasionally) P_0 and P_3. The significance of I_6 is apparent right from the outset as the movement opens with P_6 and I_6 row forms; the octave/unison statements by all the strings focus greater attention on P_6.

2. A form of a retrograde version of P_6. In essence, the ordered pitch-class intervals of the P form of the row are inverted: instead of the ordered pitch-class intervals from RP_6 (i.e., A – (10) – G – (1) – A♭ – (7) – E♭ – (7) – B♭ – (7) – etc.), this particular retrograde contains the

ordered pitch-class intervals of (2) – (11) – (5) – (5) – etc. Note that the first pitch-class of the row is D, not A.

3. A P_6 version of the row rotated to begin on the fourth order position, i.e., D♭. The choice of order position is not arbitrary, but related to the next row.

4. A row that is used extensively throughout rotation two combines attributes of both P and I row forms. Specifically, this particular row begins with the first three order positions of P_6—i.e., F♯,E,F—but then is altered to use the ordered pitch-class intervals from the I row for the remaining nine pitch classes.

5. A rotated version of P_6 that begins on the eighth-order position, so that two perfect fourth intervals initiate the row presentation. This particular row is reserved exclusively for the horn.

Notes

1. For a précis of a theory that generates relationships between harmonies and rhythms based upon both pitch- and rhythm-contour motives, see: Elizabeth West Marvin, "A Generalized Theory of Musical Contour: Its Application to Melodic and Rhythmic Analysis of Non-Tonal Music and its Perceptual and Pedagogical Implications" (Ph.D. dissertation: University of Rochester, 1988).

2. The third movement ends with a glaring notational error in the published score. Specifically, although the clarinet is notated in accordance with a transposed score throughout the work, in mm. 72–73 the solo clarinet line that serves as a transitional melody to the fourth movement is notated at concert pitch—i.e., a Major 2nd lower than as expected.

Chapter 6

The Last Temptations

Kokkonen's sole opera *The Last Temptations* is unquestionably the most successful Finnish opera of all time: with over three hundred performances to date, the only opera that has approached it in popularity is Leevi Madetoja's *Pohjalaisia* (*The Ostrobothnians*). However, Madetoja's work predates Kokkonen's by fifty years, making the reception history of Kokkonen's opera all the more impressive. In addition, *The Last Temptations* is the most performed Finnish opera outside of Finland—foreign performances of the work have occurred in Berlin, London, New York, Oslo, Stockholm, Wiesbaden and Zürich.

Historical Background

The central character of the opera is the Finnish Revivalist leader Paavo Ruotsalainen (1777–1852), arguably the most important evangelist in Finland during the first half of the nineteenth century, and who may be credited for establishing a revivalist movement that by the close of the nineteenth century was one of the largest of its kind in Finland. Born in rural north eastern Finland into a poor family, Ruotsalainen became a traveling evangelist as a young man and found a sympathetic audience with rural peasants who found his prophesizing of Christian beliefs a form of compensation for their hard day to day existence.

During Ruotsalainen's life, the Lutheran church was the official religious authority in Finland. One movement opposed to the church's power was known as the "Pietists"; the group's biggest influence was felt in the region of Savo, in the east of Finland and home of Ruotsalainen. Not surprisingly, the Pietists were targeted by the Lutheran church and the educated circles as dangerous—Ruotsalainen's ardor for preaching, in particular, led to many conflicts with the authorities. However, perhaps more than challenging the official doctrine of the Lutheran church, the Pietists in their own way contributed to an active "grass roots" movement, one that developed a pride in Finnish culture and which set the stage for the enormous wave of nationalism throughout the century (Elias Lönnrot's publication in 1835 of the important Finnish folk epic *The Kalevala*, for instance, is one obvious outcome from this movement).

The Play and Libretto

The libretto for *The Last Temptations* is based upon the 1959 play by the same title and authored by Kokkonen's second cousin, the playwright Lauri Kokkonen (1918–1985). Kokkonen was immediately attracted to the play as the basis for an opera; however, the impetus to ultimately compose the work took place fourteen years later in 1972 with a joint commission from the Nordic opera houses. The opera was completed in 1975 and premiered in Helsinki on 2 September 1975.

Although the play contains a unity and particular structure that is well-suited for a musical composition, Kokkonen labored with his second cousin to shape it into a workable libretto. For instance, not only was the play shortened—only about twenty percent of it was ultimately used—but scenes and events were re-organized to provide a different time-line to the narrative. One important change was the addition of the character Juhana, the son of Paavo and his first wife Riitta: while Juhana's death is only mentioned in the play, the character plays an important supporting role in act one of the opera. The decision to add Juhana prompted the librettist to add an additional scene not originally in the play—act one – scene five.

The opera is in two acts: act one contains eight scenes; act two, six scenes. The two acts correspond with two central aspects of Ruotsalainen's life: act one deals with his relationship with Riitta—their first encounter, first homestead, family and personal struggles; act two contains some of Ruotsalainen's conflicts between a hostile society and his religious ideas. An orchestral interlude connects every scene; the material for these interludes is not independent from the narrative but gleaned directly from the opera and, as such, plays an important role in establishing the psychological mood of the work. Like Berg's opera *Wozzeck*, each scene is a vignette onto itself, dealing with a particular time and event. Further, aside from Paavo's two monologues (one from each act), the opera contains no arias.

The rearrangement of the scenes generates a certain dramatic stability in the opera. For instance, two scenes of extreme tension—act one – scene four, where we find out that Paavo's and Riitta's child was killed during a struggle to fight a frost that threatened their existence, and act one – scene six, where Paavo, leaving on another religious sojourn, takes the last loaf of bread in their house and so angers Riitta that she throws an axe at him—are mediated by a light-hearted scene, where a capricious Juhanna announces to Riitta his ambitions to leave home to encounter adventure. In addition, in act two, the two large "group" events of the court (scene one) and graduation ceremony (scene three) are mediated by Paavo's monologue in scene two.

Although the characters are based upon real people, the events described in the opera are generalized, largely for dramatic purposes. The characters include:

* Paavo Ruotsalainen (1777–1852): a Finnish preacher
* Riitta Ruotsalainen (1779–1833): Paavo's first wife
* Anna Loviisa (1802–1880): Paavo's second wife
* Juhana Ruotsalainen (1809–1830): Paavo's and Riitta's child
* Albertiina Nenonen (1824–1905): a servant
* Jaakko Högman (1753–1806): a blacksmith who was largely responsible for introducing Paavo to his religious beliefs
* Three women: various roles in the opera, but ultimately, the daughters of Ruotsalainen
* Three men: various roles in the opera, but ultimately, the sons-in-law of Ruotsalainen

Musical Attributes

Musical Language

Like most of Kokkonen's other post-1957 compositions, *The Last Temptations* combines dodecaphonic techniques with tertian sonorities. At times, these triads provide harmonic support for the various rows deployed—an example is the consistent triadic harmonization of the twelve-tone row that appears in act one – scene one and is replicated throughout the opera, where the uppermost pitch of each triad doubles the dodecaphonically generated melody line. While the opera's various tone rows and associated harmonizations will be identified in the synopsis below, a greater percentage of the work uses tertian sonorities independent of dodecaphonic construction. As is found in countless of his other works, such harmonies are melodically associated, where successive chords in these progressions frequently contain root relationships of seconds and (especially) thirds.

One interesting feature of the opera is the numerous recurring motives and harmonies: these musical elements are consistently associated with some of the above-listed characters as well as with certain objects that are integral to the narrative. These Leitmotives function primarily to generate a mood during a scene (although it should be noted that at times they represent the source of pitch material from which vocal lines are generated). Importantly, these Leitmotives are also the material from which the various interludes of the opera are generated, engendering a vital emotional value to them that extends beyond the dramatic plot.

The various Leitmotives will be identified in the scene-by scene précis of the opera that follows this introduction; however, one recurring thematic feature that warrants discussion at this juncture is the chorale hymn "Sinuhun turvaan Jumala" ("Under your protection, O Lord"). The chorale is not original—rather, as Pekka Hako notes, the melody is an assemblage of four different chorales from the Piestist's Book of Psalms.[1] The chorale plays a vital role in the opera: not only do portions of the chorale tune appear throughout the work, but the chorale also appears three times in its entirety: in act one – scene one, in the interlude between act two – scene one and scene two, and in act two – scene six. The harmonization and orchestration is different in each instance—in fact, the modality of the chorale's final appearance even changes, adding an important emotional element to the concluding measures of the opera.

Performance Demands

Central to the opera is the role of Paavo, written for, and first championed by, the great Finnish bass Marti Talvela (1935–89). The role is grueling: Paavo is on stage for every scene of the two-hour opera except for the aforementioned act one – scene five, where only Riitta and Juhana are present. In fact, Talvela considered the role of Paavo to be one of the most difficult in the literature—comparable to Boris Godounov, a role for which Talvela was also celebrated during his career.

The Last Temptations is scored for a rather modest-sized orchestra: double woodwinds (along with a bass clarinet), four horns, three trumpets and trombones, harp, celesta and the normal complement of strings. There are two percussionists needed for the thirteen percussion instruments. There is no pre-recorded tape or live electronics required. The orchestration, for all its brilliance and demands placed upon the players is, in fact, used rather conservatively—for instance, there are no extended techniques and the percussion section is used to enrich the melodic material of the work and not as an independent section.

Adaptations of the Opera

With the opera's success, there were requests made of Kokkonen to generate arrangements of excerpts from the work; in total there are four. Unquestionably, the most important adaptation is the Four Interludes from *The Last Temptations* from 1977; in a way, the title is a misnomer, as only one of the movements is actually an interlude from the opera. The opening movement is the energetic interlude that separates act one – scenes one and two. Movements two through four are (in order) instrumental renditions of the complete act one – scene two, act one – scene six, and act one – scene eight. The Four Interludes is scored for the same size of orchestra as the opera, with instrumental lines serving the role of the various voices. The work was premiered on 27 September 1977; Okko Kamu conducted the Finnish Radio Symphony Orchestra for the performance.

Always on the look out for concert vocal repertoire, in 1974 Marti Talvela approached Kokkonen to make slight adjustments to the orchestral material of the two monologues from the opera so that they could be performed as stand-alone arias. Kokkonen completed the task in 1975 and the Two Monologues from *The Last Temptations* was premiered on 14 September 1976 by Talvela; like the Four Interludes, Okko Kamu conducted the Finnish Radio Symphony Orchestra for the performance.

Finally, there are two arrangements of "Paavo's Hymn." The first dates from 1978 and is scored for wind orchestra; the second arrangement was made in 1980 and is scored for baritone solo, children's choir and chamber ensemble.

Reception of *The Last Temptations*

For all its celebrated strengths, it is difficult to understand why *The Last Temptations* has achieved its legendary status in such a short time. While the initial success of the opera may have been bolstered by the growing wave of interest in new opera that appeared in Finland during the 1970s, the unabated popularity of Kokkonen's opera places it in a category even beyond the operas by such celebrated figures as Sallinen and Rautavaara, composers who garnered significant fame of their own during this time period. Certainly, the subject matter of Ruotsalainen's life is nondescript; and while most of the scenes have a historical background, the events described within them have been embellished to a large degree. The majority of the opera deals with Paavo's delirious dreams—in effect, only the opening and final scenes, i.e., the two that deal with Paavo's death-bed, involve the real world; the remaining twelve scenes depict his dreams about various events and people in his life. On a fundamental level, then, the opera is about Ruotsalainen's imminent death and his need to deal with two looming issues. First, was his life work of preaching the word of God worth his many travails? In other words, was he right or wrong to have undertaken his lifelong mission to God? Second, how did his actions affect his relationships with others? It is clear that Paavo suffers tremendous guilt for the misery he caused Riitta by abandoning her and the family to undertake his numerous journeys to Finland's rural areas and feels responsible for both Riitta's and Juhana's deaths. And while Paavo finds out in act one that Riitta and Juhana have entered heaven, for a large portion of the opera Paavo despairs that he cannot join them: in his mind he remains a sinner and must continue to propagate the "true" word of God— even though Riitta offers numerous prayers of thanksgiving and kindness to the contrary. A significant part of the underlying narrative, then, represents Paavo's relationship with God: if he can continue his work to save souls, his personal demons of despair—the ultimate of which, of course, is his anguish over Riitta's and Juhana's deaths—can be rationalized.

The questions that Paavo poses to himself, however, ultimately extend far beyond the framework of the opera's narrative. Indeed, these are questions that all humanity must face—namely, have the efforts of our lives had meaning and how have we touched other humans? By the end of the opera, Paavo recognizes that he must face the Gates of Heaven and be judged by his life's successes and failures as they stand. The fact that Paavo's ultimate fate is not revealed at the opera's conclusion represents a fascinating dramatic twist: ultimately, only Paavo himself can answer these fundamental questions of life, just as we the audience can only assess our own individual lives. Like all great art, the work does not provide answers to complex questions but, rather, challenges our very makeup and stimulates further thought and self-examination long after we have left the opera house.

Survey of the Opera

Act One – Scene One

The opera opens with a stormy winter night. Paavo tosses about agitatedly; he is on his deathbed. He calls out for Riitta, his first wife, although she has been dead for several years. The servant Albertiina hails Paavo's second wife Anna for help.

Much of the opening section is based upon the twelve-tone row shown
in Figure 6.1 (the black noteheads represent its typical triadic
harmonization). Although the row is partitioned into two hexachords, the
first five pitches and order positions 6–10 are retrograde inversions of each
other (i.e., F,F♯,E,G,A♭ is a retrograde and inverted row form of
E♭,D,B,C♯,C), a feature that Kokkonen exploits frequently. The agitation of
Paavo's state is musically represented by the numerous flourishes of the
row, cast in thirty-second and sextuplet-sixteenth note rhythms and at a
variety of dynamic levels.

Figure 6.1 Row form of *The Last Temptations*, act one – scene one

Albertiina brings Anna onto the stage and the two engage in a spoken
dialogue: their conversation provides the audience with some background
to Paavo, Riitta and Riitta's relationship with Paavo's children.

The agitated opening gives way to a more subdued central section:
although sextuplet-sixteenth note figures continue to appear, the majority of
the figures are now cast in eighth and quarter notes. One new feature is a
version of the twelve-tone row harmonized with triads. Importantly, all the
figures that appear in the central section are played, for the most part, at a
mezzo-piano or *piano* dynamic level, thereby allowing the spoken dialogue
to predominate.

As a means to comfort Paavo, Albertiina and Anna decide to sing a
hymn: their duet is the principal chorale melody of the opera, often referred
to as "Paavo's Hymn" (the complete chorale with its first harmonization is
shown in Figure 6.2). Paavo recognizes the tune and sings along. Now
fully conscious, he berates them and orders them out of his room.
Albertiina and Anna leave the stage and the curtain falls to the first
interlude.

Interlude One

The twelve-tone row that served as the basis for scene one permeates the
first interlude. The row is used by itself melodically both as a baseline and
the uppermost voice; it frequently appears harmonized with the same series
of triads illustrated in Figure 6.1.

The ternary-designed interlude begins aggressively and at a *fortissimo*
dynamic level with a series of row statements that are realized largely by

the brass and harmonized by tertian sonorities (also by the brass); the strings and woodwinds play numerous neighbor note figures as background support for these various row statements.

Figure 6.2 *The Last Temptations*, **act one, mm. 110–128**
      (piano/vocal reduction)

By m. 153 the dynamic level has diminished to *pianissimo*, demarcating the central section. Of primary importance is a succession of three harmonic dyads played by the woodwinds and associated via contrary melodic motion. And while the supporting material for these harmonic dyads is, like the opening section, also a number of neighbor-note figures derived from the primary twelve-tone row, these neighbor figures are cast in a variety of rhythmic patterns, adding a sense of agitation to the central section.

The dynamic level and orchestral density gradually increase throughout the central section, leading to the orchestral tutti in m. 165. The return to the twelve-tone row harmonized in triads and played by the brass at a *fortissimo* dynamic level marks the return to the opening section, rounding off the ternary design. Numerous statements of the harmonized version of the twelve-tone row appear for the remainder of the interlude. However, with each successive realization of the row, the dynamic level gradually decreases, leading to the final sonority of the interlude—a sustained bitonal chord of C Major and E♭ Major, played at a quadruple *piano* dynamic level.

Versions of this interlude appear two further times in the opera: between act two – scenes three and four and act two – scenes five and six. In all three instances, the music depicts the transition from Paavo's consciousness (reality) and unconscious (dream) states.

Act One – Scene Two

The prior interlude has transported us from the reality of the opening scene to Paavo's dream world. The scene is a country dance where Paavo and Riitta first met. Three men and three women mock Paavo and warn Riitta to ignore him, for they claim Paavo will bring her a lifetime of misery. Despite their warnings, Riitta decides to leave with Paavo and encourage him and his life of ministry.

The scene is a rondo design. A feature that permeates the scene is the realization of the fourteen-note row shown in Figure 6.3a, labeled the "Dancing" leitmotive (shown in Figure 6.3b). Of note are the frequent meter changes, a feature that pervades the scene.

The refrain restates the melodic and metric features from the introduction. The three men and women sing about Paavo's silly dancing and Riitta's sadness. Riitta runs towards Paavo and they begin to reminisce.

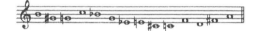

Figure 6.3a Row form of *The Last Temptations*, act one – scene two

Figure 6.3b *The Last Temptations*, act one, mm. 194–207
      (piano reduction)

At m. 293 the character of the music changes dramatically: the tone row from the refrain is absent, the meter is almost entirely in $\frac{2}{4}$; the texture is much more homophonic in nature; and there is an ostinato based upon the pitch F and played by the lower strings and tympani. The three men and women are now joined by an on-stage chorus (Riitta and Paavo are silent), who warn Riitta that if she remains with Paavo her life will be filled with despair and hardship.

The refrain returns at m. 331, as does the melodic material, rhythm and metric setting from the opening. Only Paavo and Riitta are heard; Paavo tries to convince Riitta to marry him, although Riitta remains skeptical.

A second episode begins at m. 359. Once again, the chorus reminds Riitta of the life of misery she will have to endure with Paavo and tries to encourage her to stay away from him. As with the first episode, the texture becomes more homophonic in character than the refrain and maintains an ostinato upon A♭ (mm. 359–371) and (predominantly) C from mm. 373–389.

The final refrain begins at m. 390. The melodic and rhythmic features from the prior refrains return; however, Paavo and Riitta are absent and instead the chorus continue to warn Riitta about the life of misery she will bear with Paavo.

With the postlude beginning at m. 439, Riitta has decided to join Paavo. She tells him, however, that she must visit Jaako Högman, the blacksmith who introduced Paavo to his first religious beliefs, providing a segue to the next scene.

Interlude II

The second interlude is a ternary form design. The outer parts (mm. 517–534 and mm. 538–541) are characterized by numerous statements of the tertian-harmonized version of the twelve-tone row used in both scene one and interlude one; an ostinato played by the tympani, harp and lower strings underlies the various row statements.

In the short middle part, the first five pitches from the row (i.e., E♭,D,B,C♯,C) are used as an inner-voice ostinato and support the first six pitches of Paavo's Hymn, played by the tubular bells in long note values; the timbre anticipates its prominent use in the next scene.

Act One – Scene Three

Riitta and Paavo enter the home of the blacksmith Högman. The sonority shown in Figure 6.4, labeled the "Blacksmith" leitmotive, appears throughout the scene; the leitmotive is distinguished by its similar recurring orchestration of brass and low woodwind registers.

Figure 6.4 "Blacksmith" leitmotive

Riitta accuses Högman of importing false doctrines to Paavo: she complains that because of Paavo's constant travels away from home, the family endured a life of misery—at times, close to starvation. Högman responds with anger: "Women are not worth arguing with over matters of doctrine ... One thing thou lackest and thereby all things—an inner knowledge of Jesus Christ."

The pitch material for much of the scene is derived from scene one's twelve-tone row; although the row appears in its original format, the order positions are frequently permuted. New, however, is a bitonal sonority that combines E, D and A Major triads; this particular sonority reappears throughout the opera and is labeled the "Heaven" leitmotive. For instance, the same sonority supports Riitta's lines towards the end of the scene ("Listen, smith: we must attack the barrier of heaven. Surely it will move at least a little, just enough for us to manage to slip inside."); the setting in mm. 687–691 is illustrated in Figure 6.5.

As the scene ends, Högman tells Riitta that she should not complain about the circumstances of her life as the Barrier of Heaven will open to those who suffer and toil; Riitta is unmoved by his claims of the afterlife; Paavo, in his first acknowledgment of guilt over his treatment of Riitta, claims that he is too weak to open the Barrier.

Figure 6.5 *The Last Temptations*, act one, mm. 687–691
(piano/vocal reduction)

Interlude III

The interlude begins with the Blacksmith leitmotive supporting a version of Paavo's Hymn melody that, interestingly, contains tritones instead of perfect 4^{ths} for its opening intervals—perhaps a musical metaphor representing Paavo's guilt identified in the prior section.

The majority of the interlude is cast at a tempo ($\downarrow$= 63–68) and character that typifies the following scene. Of import, however, is a series of triads that continually repeats as a type of chaconne, over which a variety of melodies appears; as we shall presently see, the chaconne is of significance in the next scene.

Act One – Scene Four

Riitta and Paavo appear at their first homestead by the lake. They are full of optimism as they reminisce playfully about beginning a life together, while gazing in wonder at the expansiveness of the countryside and lake and the excitement of their newborn child.

This portion of the bipartite-designed scene is primarily controlled by the series of harmonies introduced in the prior interlude (Figure 6.6 illustrates this chaconne in the opening measures of the scene). There are two passages in which the chaconne is absent. The first is from mm. 830–840, in which harmonies structured primarily with perfect 5th intervals and cast in somewhat longer rhythmic values are used as musical metaphors to depict the expansiveness of the trees and lake surrounding Paavo's and Riitta's homestead. The second exception is the passage in mm. 840–859. Here, Paavo cheerfully promises to build Riitta a tall log cabin; however, a wicker gate reminds him of his unfulfilled promise and once again of the Barrier of Heaven which he dare not cross. A new, "Frost" leitmotive appears briefly during Paavo's momentary anxiety; its presence at this moment of the narrative engenders a subtle foreboding of the tragedy that unfolds in the second part of the scene. An arrhythmic version of the Frost leitmotive, along with the countermelody frequently associated with it, is illustrated in Figure 6.7; both are constructed from the same octatonic collection, OCT$_{1,2}$.

Figure 6.6 *The Last Temptations*, act one, mm. 791–805
   (piano/vocal reduction)

Figure 6.7 Pitches of "Frost" leitmotive and its countermelody
   (arrhythmic version)

A bass ostinato beginning at m. 923 completely alters the character of the music and initiates the second part of the scene. Here, much of the narrative is presented by the three men, three women and chorus. They relate how Paavo's and Riitta's optimism is misguided for, in fact, they faced a life of misery together. We are told how a white frost came early one year: although they desperately fought to save their crops, in the end Riitta and Paavo not only lost their harvest but also their infant child. The Frost leitmotive and its countermelody permeate every aspect of this portion of the scene, from the orchestral melodies to the lines sung by the chorus. As the tragedy unfolds, the individual choral parts become higher in register (at one point the sopranos sing a C#6) and both the vocal and orchestral lines increase in dynamic level (to triple *forte*), leading to the climatic homophonic passage in mm. 1064–1070 that ends the scene.

Interlude IV

The bipartite-designed interlude begins at a *fortissimo* dynamic level. The first part contains a series of three statements of the Frost leitmotive cast in long rhythmic values. The respective melodies are harmonized by different triads, creating a series of bitonal chord progressions.

The second part of the interlude contains an interesting dialogue between the woodwinds that introduces the primary motivic idea of the next scene, "Juhana's" leitmotive.

Act One – Scene Five

This is the one scene from the opera in which Paavo is absent. It opens with Paavo's and Riitta's son Juhana mending his father's knapsack. He sings and dances, taunting his mother about the need to leave his dreary existence and undertake a life of adventure in the wider world. Riitta retorts that she wants nothing of this life for her son and that there is much work to be done around the house. Riitta snatches the knapsack from Juhana and admonishes him for helping Paavo leave on another mission— and once again abandoning the family for an indefinite period of time.

The two motives that pervade the scene vividly capture Juhana's capricious, carefree character are illustrated in Figure 6.8 (specifically, mm. 1135–1148). The first is Juhana's leitmotive, first introduced in the preceding scene: its use is prominent in his vocal lines, either as part of the melodies sung by him or as the supporting orchestral lines. The second motive, although here appearing first in Riitta's vocal part in mm. 1139–1142, is largely used as complementary material for the numerous orchestral passages that bridge the vocal interaction between Riitta and Juhana.

The scene ends with Juhana dancing with Riitta before he runs off stage, followed by a short orchestral postlude in which both motives play a significant role.

Figure 6.8 *The Last Temptations*, act one, mm. 1135–1147
(piano/vocal reduction)

Interlude V

An ostinato-like figure, cast in a quarter-note rhythm at a tempo of ♩ = 120, pervades the interlude; it engenders a sense of urgency, one that establishes the mood for the most dramatically intense scene of act one. The basis of the ostinato is the six-note row shown in Figure 6.9a, although a T_7 transposition—i.e., E♭,D,F,E,C,C♯—appears frequently (the row is a reordering of the chromatic hexachord from the latter portion of the row from scene one). Figure 6.9b illustrates the realization of the row at the outset of the interlude.

Figure 6.9a Row form of *The Last Temptations*, act one – interlude V

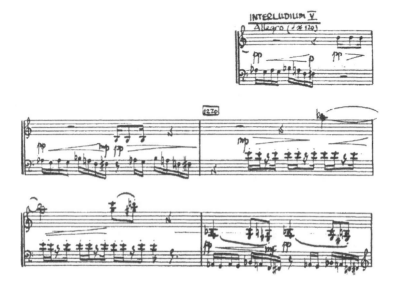

**Figure 6.9b *The Last Temptations*, act one, mm. 1218–1222
            (piano reduction)**

Act One – Scene Six

The sixth scene is the most vividly passionate in the first act. The action takes place in the same room as the preceding scene: Paavo enters and angrily demands his knapsack from Riitta. They argue: Riitta claims that Paavo is forever away from home while his family starves; Paavo retorts that she has no business interfering with him propagating the word of God. As their argument swells, the music intensifies, and leads to Riitta's threat to kill Paavo, followed by her throwing an axe at him.

The six-note row that dominated the preceding interlude forms the basis for much of the orchestra's pitch material from the scene. However, the row is extended to seven pitches through the addition of the pitch E; the inversional row form beginning on A♭—(A♭,A,F♯,G,B,B♭,C)—is also used to a large degree. While these two particular row forms generate a significant percentage of the pitch material of these ostinatos, transpositions also appear.

The two vocal parts are through-composed and not derived from either the prime or inverted row forms; in accordance with the orchestral accompaniment, however, they become more agitated in nature as the scene unfolds. Essentially, the scene is designed as a uni-dimensional crescendo, in which subtle changes throughout the scene contribute to the crescendo. As an illustration, consider the three-dyad progression that played a role in the preceding interlude: the dyad sequence first appears at m. 1307, i.e., about mid-point in the scene, and gradually becomes increasingly vital to the orchestral framework, both harmonically and texturally, for the remainder of the scene.

Monologue No. 1

Following Riittas's attempt on Paavo's life, the stage darkens, leaving only him illuminated. The remainder of the scene is the first of Paavo's two solo arias (the second occurs in act two – scene two). Paavo cries in despair for his cruel treatment of Riitta ("Riitta, Riitta, did I call you a wretched woman? ... It's me who is the wretch."). His anguish subsides as he tries to reconcile the misery that has been inflicted upon his family with the importance of spreading the word of God ("The wind whistled me beyond the mountains, towards the world of men."); a "Wandering" leitmotive, shown in Figure 6.10, first appears at m. 1332 with this particular text and plays an important role for the remainder of the monologue. Paavo ultimately questions whether his life of labor may have been in vain ("There, there was the same problem—people, people, people. I could not help them: I was talking to the air."). He remains too weak to open the Barrier to Heaven and calls out to Riitta, but he cannot find her.

Figure 6.10 "Wandering" leitmotive

Although the monologue is through-composed, there are two important cadential gestures—one at the mid-point, the other at the conclusion, suggesting a bipartite design.   Although the vocal lines and harmonic support are different in both instances, the two cadences are associated by: (1) the phrases that ultimately lead to these gestures feature the "Wandering" leitmotive prominently; (2) a similar gradual increase in dynamic level from *piano* to *fortissimo* in these two phrases; and (3) a gradual accumulation of orchestral texture in these two phrases leading to the final tutti chords employing the entire orchestra. One further similarity is the sixteenth-note sextuplet flourish that immediately follows the tutti chords of both cadential gestures. The twelve-element figure is played by the solo flute and violin and engenders an important dynamic and textural contrast after the ending tutti chords. (In point of fact, though, the solo flourish appears throughout the monologue and functions consistently as a type of codetta figure to numerous other vocal phrases. However, the degree of contrast, as regards dynamic and orchestral texture, between the two aforementioned tutti chords and twelve-element flourishes is particularly noteworthy.)

Figure 6.11 *The Last Temptations*, act one, mm. 1504–1511
              (piano reduction)

Interlude VI

The interlude is a bipartite design.   Part one contains a rhythmically augmented version of the "Wandering" leitmotive played by the strings. Part two (mm. 1504–1511, illustrated in Figure 6.11) contains the significant pitch and rhythmic motives from scene seven (the motive in its characteristic realization first appears in m. 1505). Although its role is not significant here, the minor 3rd interval in mm. 1507–1508 becomes a vital motivic element for the choral parts in the following scene.

Act One – Scene Seven

The scene centers predominantly on Riitta. Village women (the chorus) enter the house and taunt Riitta; in a roundabout way they tell her that Juhana has been murdered. The women wonder why Riitta does not morn for Juhana; she replies that she has already wept for him for three years. Paavo has been listening to Riitta from the side of the stage; in his anguish over Juhana he cries that all his life God has scourged him with an iron whip and that he has deserved it.

The scene is a ternary form. Part A contains interaction between the women's chorus and Riitta. Several motives are significant: (1) a descending scalar line that ends with repetition of a minor 3rd interval; (2) a descending contour related to motive (1), but that ends with a descending perfect 4th; and (3) an ascending four-note figure. Although not a pitch motive like these three, a further important element is the numerous repeated notes that permeate the musical landscape.

Part B is short—from m. 1555 to 1567—and features only Riitta. Not only is the somewhat whimsical character from part A significantly altered, but, in addition, none of the motives that distinguished the opening part are used. The dynamically subdued and rhythmically augmented melodic lines by both the strings and Riitta add a somewhat pensive quality when she questions the women about their concern over Juhana's whereabouts and well-being.

The nature of the rhythmic and melodic motives from the opening part A return at m. 1568, and lead to the dramatic climax of the scene—the announcement of Juhana's death in mm. 1585 to 1588. The dissonances from the passage give way to the final section of the scene, Paavo's anguish over Juhana's death.

Interlude VII

The character of act one's final interlude could not contrast more with the preceding scene: the numerous dissonances and short, repetitive and capricious rhythmic motives have given way to a slow, chorale-styled texture played predominantly by the strings at a *piano* dynamic level. The four motives that generate the pitch material of the interlude are illustrated in Figure 6.12. Motive one is a series of five harmonic dyads (mm. 1638–1640); motive two is the opening five pitches of the row ordering from scene one, only harmonized with triads (mm. 1641–1643); motive three is a series of harmonies in which an ascending baseline is set against a series of triads whose uppermost voice descends in contour (mm. 1644–1647); and motive four is the harmonic progression that concludes the interlude (mm. 1648–1649). The latter motive is labeled the "Opening of Heaven's Gate" leitmotive; the harmonic progression appears frequently with Riitta's entrance into heaven in the next scene, as well as throughout act two.

Figure 6.12 *The Last Temptations*, **act one, mm. 1638–1649**
          (piano reduction)

Act One – Scene Eight

Three years have passed since Juhana's death; Riitta is now dying. She is at peace and in her final hours fondly recalls with Paavo the idyllic setting of their first homestead together on the island. Riitta's lack of anger surprises Paavo: after all her grief, how can Riitta give thanks when he cannot? As a final request, she asks Paavo to recite a hymn of thanksgiving. As he sings, Juhana joins in. Riitta rises from her deathbed and walks toward her son: "Now the Gate is open."

The calm and serene mood of the final scene is matched by one of the most exquisite musical settings in all of Kokkonen's oeuvre. The four motives from the preceding interlude represent a significant amount of the pitch material in the scene (it should be noted that the "Opening of Heaven's Gate" leitmotive, which was played by the strings in the preceding interlude, is now reserved for the brass). The four motives are never heard simultaneously, but, rather, follow one another in succession; in addition to the flow of harmony, the four motives play a significant role in directing the pitch material of the vocal lines. The scene ends calmly with two leitmotives: the "Opening of Heaven's Gate," followed immediately by a sustained statement of the "Heaven" leitmotive played by the entire orchestra.

Act Two – Scene One (Nine)

Three men appear at a court where Paavo once had to defend himself against charges of challenging the official authority of the Lutheran church; they devise a plot to confound Paavo in order to confront his arrogance. The seven-note motive shown in Figure 6.13 pervades the scene; the melody is virtually always played by the strings and serves as the basis for a significant number of the vocal melodies.

**Figure 6.13 *The Last Temptations*, act two, mm. 1–6
(piano reduction)**

The three men feed Paavo's insecurities by humiliating him and taunt him with seductive dancing women: this particular section is accompanied by robust dance music and exhilarating choral writing that gradually construct the scene to a thrilling climax, one that ends with Paavo collapsing in despair. The scene ends with his poignant cry of "O Son of God, have mercy on me, a sinner"—an admission of guilt that even he, a man thoroughly consumed by the word of God, is not impervious to "earthly" sins.

Interlude I (VIII)

As a means to answer Paavo's despair that concluded the previous scene, the chorus sings an a cappella unison version of "Paavo's Hymn."

Act Two – Scene Two (Ten)

Riitta appears and once again calls Paavo to the island. He replies that he cannot, and in his second monologue insists that he still has much work left to reform the Finnish people. ("I have yet, before I die, to speak to the Finnish people. Do I have to speak? I have to, for I've been called. Into the sea of men I cast a net all flaming: with it I search for sinful wretches.")

The monologue is a ternary form. The outer parts are distinguished by numerous modal inflections and Kokkonen's frequent association of harmonies through Major and minor 3rd relationships. The contrasting middle part, mm. 335–353, is distinguished by a broader range in Paavo's vocal line. Further, the thirty-second note flourishes that initiate each of the three phrases, combined with the unmeasured tremolos that support the vocal lines, engender a quality of panache to the middle, a musical setting that superbly captures the sense of exuberance and urgency from the text ("If the fire of the World still could touch the feelings and fill the heart with trembling and ecstasy, then I'd speak as though to men, whom I would see for the last time").

The scene ends with Riitta asking Paavo to not undertake any further journeys, but, instead, to accompany her to the island. Paavo counters, however, that he cannot do so yet, for "The Christianity of reason must be crushed in its lair." He is invited to speak at a festival in Helsinki and intends to convert a number of people to his teachings (the "Wandering" leitmotive features prominently as supportive material to Paavo's lines).

Interlude II (IX)

This brief interlude is a ternary form. In part A, mm. 400–403, the primary melodic material is played by the English horn and is derived from the twelve-tone row from act one – scene one. Part B (mm. 404–406) contains the initial portion of "Paavo's Hymn," played by the strings. The remainder of the interlude (mm. 407–413) once again utilizes the twelve-tone row from act one – scene one, again played by the English horn; however, the tone row is now harmonized with triads using other woodwinds and the strings.

Act Two – Scene Three (Eleven)

The scene is a university graduation ceremony. A seven-note row in mm. 420–421 played by the woodwinds and strings provides a significant amount of the accompanimental melodic material; it also serves as the basis for some of the vocal lines. A distinctive rhythm associated with the row pervades the scene. Figure 6.14 illustrates the opening seven measures (mm. 420–426); of note is the transpositional relationship between the motives in mm. 422–423 and mm. 424–425, an association that prevails throughout the scene.

Paavo wants to enter the ceremony as an invited guest; however the three men and three women stop him, declaring that an uneducated farmer has no business to be part of such a service. Paavo argues that they are wrong: he is a learned man because he has studied religious tracts since he was a boy. The men and woman demand that he name the titles of these books; when Paavo complies, they taunt him by claiming that such books do not even exist. In the midst of the mocking (at m. 518 the chorus has joined the three men and three woman in the jeering), Paavo suddenly hears a brass procession play a version of his hymn. He halts it and attempts to address the collection of academics and clergy from the procession ("Comfort ye, comfort ye, my people. Great is heaven and earth. Believe ye, hope ye, love ye."); his words of praise to God are supported by a sustained version of the "Heaven" leitmotive played by the strings. They ignore him and when Paavo tries to follow the Bishop of the North (the brass procession version of "Paavo's Hymn" reappears), he is restrained. Paavo wrestles himself free, then suddenly looses interest in the proceedings and cries out in despair ("Lord Jesus Christ, O Son of God, have mercy on me, a sinner").

Interlude III (X)

The interlude is in two parts. In part one, a variation of the first interlude from act one returns (i.e., the music that depicted the transition from the reality of the first scene to the dream world that has occupied the opera's narrative since act one – scene two). As before, the row ordering from the opening scene dominates: statements of the row played by the brass are harmonized with triads and are supported by numerous string ostinatos that are either generated from short fragments of the primary row form or transpositions of it. The association with the first interlude is unmistakable and at first implies that the opera is being transported back to the reality state of the opening. However, the character of the music changes from the violent triple *forte* swirls of ostinatos at m. 623 to the second part of the interlude: a calm, four-measure adagio passage cast at a *piano* dynamic level; the latter passage, shown in Figure 6.15, contains the primary pitch material for the next scene.

Figure 6.14 *The Last Temptations*, act two, mm. 419–426
(piano/vocal reduction)

Figure 6.15 *The Last Temptations*, act two, mm. 622–627
(piano reduction)

Significantly, the next scene remains a dream for Paavo. The
interlude, then, can be interpreted in two ways: (1) Paavo attempts to regain
consciousness (part one of the interlude) but has not yet done so (part two),

or (2) that Paavo did briefly regain consciousness during the initial portion of the interlude, but immediately slipped back to a delirious dream state.

Act Two – Scene Four (Twelve)

Riitta once again calls Paavo to the island. Although full of doubt, in the end he believes that he will be let in ("I am coming as a troubled man and a wretched sinner, to be the lowest step.").

This scene, a duet between Riitta and Paavo on an empty stage, is the briefest of the fourteen from the opera, even with the *adagio* tempo indication of ♪ = 80. A significant portion of the pitch material in the dialogue is generated from the series of harmonies of the chaconne that played a prominent role in the first half of act one – scene four (i.e., the scene describing Riitta's and Paavo's first homestead).

Interlude IV (XI)

Like interlude VIII, a vocal part dominates. In response to Paavo thoughts from the previous scene of joining Riitta at the island, she offers a prayer of thanksgiving ("He forgiveth all thy sins: and healeth all thine infirmities ...").

The character of the music from the previous scene, as regards the melodic material and harmonic progressions, is retained. However, a sustained bitonal chord adds further harmonic support of the melodic material: although the pitches are slightly different, the chord is evocative of the "Heaven" leitmotive.

Act Two – Scene Five (Thirteen)

The mood from the prior scene remains: the stage is empty, with only Paavo's face now visible; nobody looks at each other in this suspended, timeless ambiance. Paavo prays for forgiveness ("O thou of all most merciful, crucified Lord Jesus Christ, have mercy on me, a troubled sinner"). The blacksmith Jaakko Högman returns and suggests a prayer of encouragement; his leitmotive appears throughout the passage. Riitta next appears, and offers a prayer of thanksgiving; the melodic and harmonic material based upon the material from the previous scene forms the basis of her prayer. Finally, Juhana emerges, accompanied by the "Juhana" Leitmotive, and sings the Lord's Prayer. The time has come for Paavo to settle his accounts, and he is prepared for the consequences ("Let the Lord carry out his business; this is my portion").

Interlude V (XII)

The music from interlude III (X) returns. However, not only is the present passage slightly longer than interlude III, but it also employs a greater percentage of the orchestra (the piccolo flourishes, for instance, add a particular level of brilliance) and ultimately reaches a quadruple *forte* dynamic level. The interlude ends with the brass procession version of "Paavo's Hymn" that played a role in act two – scene three.

Act Two – Scene Six (Fourteen)

We have returned to the reality state of the opera, using the same stage setup as the opening of the opera—i.e., Paavo is on his death bed and Albertiina and Anna tend to him during his final hours. The brass procession music from the end of the previous interlude serves to open the final scene. Paavo tosses about in his bed and shouts for the Bishop of the North to wait for him (a reference to act two – scene three). As he comes out of his delirium, Paavo recognizes that he is surrounded by his three daughters and their respective husbands and that, in fact, it has been these six individuals who have tormented him in his dreams throughout the opera. This particular passage from the opening of the scene is notable, as a number of the leitmotives that played a significant role earlier in the opera are recapitulated. He now recognizes that his time has come: he asks to ensure that his affairs are in order and then requests that Albertiina read his favorite prayer. Paavo then sings the first verse of "Paavo's Hymn," but becomes silent for the remainder of it—a version of the hymn sung in unison by the eight characters and accompanied by the full orchestra. Notably, it is the one time in the opera that the hymn is cast in the Major mode. The change in mode is remarkable: in the final measures, Paavo sings praise to God as he sinks into death and approaches the gate, believing that he has prevailed; the Major mode flavor of the hymn metaphorically supports Paavo's conviction. However, in a remarkable dramatic touch, the ending is left ambiguous: we are never told whether the Gate to Heaven is actually opened for Paavo—significantly, the "Opening of Heaven's Gate" leitmotive is conspicuously absent—and instead, the opera ends calmly on a sustained E Major triad.

Note

1.　See Pekka Hako, liner notes from compact disc recording of Joonas Kokkonen, *The Last Temptations* (Finlandia, FACD 104).

Chapter 7

Vocal Works

Of the nineteen compositions written between the 1936 *Etude in a Classical Style* for piano solo and the 1957 *Music for String Orchestra*, almost half (eight) are for voice and piano; all are relatively short in duration. Given the importance placed upon art song during his early career, the paucity of post-1957 vocal pieces in Kokkonen's oeuvre (roughly a quarter) is surprising—and especially given his life-long attraction towards poetry. In total there are only twelve vocal works (thirteen if the opera *The Last Temptations* is included); all but three are either for solo chorus, chorus with orchestra, or the singular work for soloist and orchestra, *The Hades of the Birds*. Further, aside from *The Last Temptations*, only the *Hades of the Birds* and the Requiem at all approach the rigor of such orchestral works as the four symphonies or chamber pieces such as three string quartets. In short, while vocal music remained a part of Kokkonen's mature works, his interest turned towards larger ensembles, and the more intimate vocal forms that occupied a central position in his early years as a composer clearly took a secondary role to his expanded canvases of instrumental music.

About half of Kokkonen's pre-1957 works for voice remain unpublished; to date, only one song has been recorded. Although charming in their own right, most are relatively straight forward harmonically and are virtually devoid of any formal sophistication. In short, while these immature works can provide an image of Kokkonen's early compositional style, they are insufficient to illustrate the evolution to Kokkonen's watershed work, the *Music for String Orchestra*—especially when compared with more advanced compositions from the same time period such as the 1948 Piano Trio or 1955 *Duo* for violin and piano.

In sum, this chapter examines only a small percentage of the vocal works from Kokkonen's oeuvre. None of the early songs will be discussed, and only two works for voice and piano, the 1955 *Illat* and *Sub Rosa* from 1973, merit minor attention. Two a cappella choral works, the 1963 *Missa a cappella* and 1966 *Laudatio Domini*, and the 1970 cantata *Erekhtheion* warrant slightly longer discussion. Finally, the two most extensive sections of the chapter contain discussion of the 1958 orchestral song cycle *The Hades of the Birds* and the 1980 Requiem.

Illat

These three short songs for soprano and piano were written in 1955, the same year as the *Duo* for violin and piano; the titles are "Hiljainen, surullinen ilta" ("A Calm, Tragic Evening"), "Ihana, surullinen ilta" ("A Wonderful, Tragic Evening"), and "Kevätilta" ("Spring's Evening"). The texts are based upon three poems by the Finnish poet Katri Vala.

Like the *Duo*, there is a decreased reliance upon tertian sonorities in *Illat*, when compared with Kokkonen's earlier works from the 1940s and 1950s. Instead, a significant amount of the melodic material for both the vocal lines and piano is generated via intervallic associations—and in particular, from six- to eight-note motives. While the work does not by any means contain the sophisticated dodecaphonic organization that would come to characterize Kokkonen's compositions a few years later, the pervasive use of these short motives to structure many of the themes and harmonies in *Illat* makes it a valuable companion study with the *Music for String Orchestra*, Kokkonen's first work containing dodecaphonic procedures. As an illustration to the compositional approach in *Illat*, consider Figure 7.1, the opening fifteen measures from the first song: of note is the extensive manipulation of a seven-note motive {C,B,G,B♭,A♭,E♭,E} (note that the vocal line is a T₇ transposition of this motive).

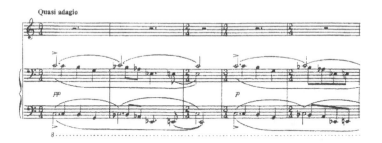

Figure 7.1 *Illat*, "Hiljainen, surullinen ilta," mm. 1–17

Figure 7.1, continued

Lintujen tuonela (*The Hades of the Birds*)

Kokkonen's song cycle *The Hades of the Birds*, for mezzo-soprano and orchestra, dates from 1958 and is the composer's first work scored for a full orchestra. The second song, from which the title of the composition is derived, was the first of the three to be completed. The origins of the work are somewhat unusual. In early September of 1958 Kokkonen was informed that he was the recipient of the Wihuri Foundation Scholarship and, as part of the ceremony festivities, he was to have one of his orchestral songs performed—a difficult proposition, since, apart from the recent *Music for String Orchestra*, Kokkonen could not even claim an orchestral work in his oeuvre, much less one for voice and orchestra.[1] Without informing the committee of his lack of a composition for the occasion, Kokkonen quickly set out to complete the task at hand. Work on the poem *The Hades of the Birds* by the Finnish poet P. Mustapää went quickly and the song was completed in time for the ceremony that took place on 9 October 1958. The vocal part was written for the young Finnish mezzo-soprano Raili Kostia, a recent graduate from the Sibelius Academy who had made quite a reputation during her tenure as a student; Kostia premiered the work, with Jorma Panula conducting the Finnish Radio Symphony Orchestra.

Almost from the outset, Kokkonen had plans to extend the song into a trilogy; the remaining two were written in early 1959. The entire cycle was premiered on 7 April 1959, once again with Kostia as the soloist and Panula conducting the Finnish Radio Symphony Orchestra.

"Täydellisyyden maassa" ("In the World of Perfection")

The first song is a through-composed song and cast in a two-part design. Part one is marked *Tempo di valse* and set in a ⅜ meter. The vast majority of the pitch material from this portion of the song is generated from the series of four chords that appears from the outset (Figure 7.2 displays the opening fifteen measures). The vocal melody contains no dissonant pitches—in other words, it is completely in accordance with the underlying harmony. The consistent rhythm and repeating, unambiguous triads seem to capture Kokkonen's image of the text—i.e., a land of stability, one full of beauty and miracles.

An orchestral interlude begins at m. 59; the same triadic harmonies that have dominated up to now pervade the first portion of the interlude. However, a major change in character begins at m. 75: associated with the tempo change to *Un poco piu lento* is the first dissonance of the song: a B minor triad combined simultaneously with the pitch C. The remainder of the interlude contains features that characterize part two. For instance, while the triads from part one remain, the contrasting bass line and dissonant clashes prompt a sense of harmonic ambiguity; the shift from harmonic stability to harmonic instability reflects nicely the corresponding change in text:

> I merely sensed secret things about its region.
> The wind did not sing in the trees of the forest;
> not a single bird took up its song there.

In fact, the last line of text is set with the primary melodic motive from the second movement, suggesting that the protagonist is conscious of something more sinister about the paradise identified at the outset—a supposition that is musically reinforced by the numerous dissonances during the latter portion of the song (for instance, an E pedal supporting a bitonal sonority comprised of G and B♭ Major triads).

Figure 7.2 *The Hades of the Birds*, **"In the World of Perfection,"**
mm. 1–15 (piano/vocal reduction)

"Lintujen tuonela" ("The Hades of the Birds")

We are now cast into the nightmarish world suggested during the latter portion of the previous song; a few lines of the poem provide a flavor of the text:

> And the trees are ghostly trees,
> empty and bewitched,
> and no-one can know where that country lies.
> And dead songbirds,
> with sad, rigid beaks sing in its trees.

An eighteen-measure orchestral introduction gradually unfolds the primary six-note motive, {B,B♭,C,A,G,G♯}—a re-ordered chromatic tetrachord. An ostinato pervades section one (mm. 19–74); the pitches of the ostinato can be re-ordered to generate a second chromatic tetrachord. Clearly the labored, unchanging—in a word, monochromatic—ostinato supports the images from the text: namely, that this is a road upon which one should not journey.

An orchestral interlude from measures 75 to 87 contains two motives that permeate section two: (1) a four-note figure played by the flutes and clarinets, and (2) the minor 3rd oscillation between G and B♭ by the cellos and double basses in unmeasured tremolos (additional unmeasured tremolos by the violins and tympani appear once the vocalist enters). The text from section two describes the protagonist's desolate environment:

> Oh, there, further away is the black sorrowful and immobile shoe of Oceanus.
> The moon shines in the manner of day,
> on its misty country, and the day just like the moon, and without outline the
> night is reflected in the water.

The sparse texture, the pervasive string tremolos, and seemingly random metrical placements of the four-note motive, all combine to produce an eerie sense of timelessness. The vocal line in this section continues to rely extensively upon the {B,B♭,C,A,G,G♯} hexachord from part one.

A second orchestral interlude connecting sections two and three appears in mm. 141–161; the two-part interlude is dominated by octave/unison statements of the opening cello/bass ostinato, played at a *forte* dynamic level by the violins. Part two of the interlude contains an imitative passage that features C-E♭ and B-G♯ minor 3rd dyads played by the flutes, oboes and clarinets. The interaction of these two motives anticipates their use in section three (mm. 162–185), in which all the vocal lines are based upon diminished triads (these triads underscore the text "And dead songbirds, with sad, rigid beaks sing in its trees …").

The fourth and final section begins at m. 184. The vocal melody and cello/double bass ostinato from section one return; these features support the corresponding repetition of the opening lines of text. Given the desolate nature of the content, the modal inflection to E Major comes as a welcome relief and suggests that the protagonist is safe from the distressing surroundings depicted in the song.

"Sade" ("Rain")

The pitch material of final song is generated via an interesting mélange of tertian-based sonorities and dodecaphonic procedures. However, Kokkonen's use of twelve-tone rows in *Sade* is not as extensive when compared with the dodecaphonic procedures used in *Music for String Orchestra*: aside from the twenty-measure orchestral introduction and brief interlude between the text's two strophes (mm. 61–65), the realization of the rows—for both vocalist and orchestra—is only melodically conceived and at service to the underlying tertian-styled harmonies.

The three rows used in the song are illustrated in Figure 7.3. Row B is a retrograde form of row A; row C is the inverted row form of row A beginning on E (the final two pitches are repetitions—in other words, row C is a ten-note row with duplications). Of interest is the number of order positions that remain contiguous between rows A and C (and, as a corollary, between rows B and C), generating subtle harmonic familiarity between the three rows.

Figure 7.3 Row forms of *The Hades of the Birds*, "Rain"

The song is cast in a modified strophic design: although the text is different, the musical settings between strophes are quite similar. Clearly we have left the dark world of the previous song:

> Oh happiest song which I captured—
> I could not even know half of it,
> I could only understand half of it

and a few lines later:

> I also heard the splendour of heaven ... just like a clear song.

The increased transparency in musical texture as well as the greater conformity between the rhythm and meter, when compared with *The Hades of the Birds*, underscore the changes to the character of the text and in many ways return us to the optimistic sound world that appeared at the outset of the cycle. Figure 7.4 reproduces mm. 22–30 as an illustration of how these musical attributes underline the first two lines of text (note that the vocal line contains two realizations of row A).

Figure 7.4 *The Hades of the Birds*, "Rain," mm. 17–31
(piano/vocal reduction)

Missa a cappella

Kokkonen's 1963 *Missa a cappella* is a six-voice work for soprano, mezzo-soprano, alto, tenor, baritone and bass.   The five movements of the composition contain the Ordinary of the mass—i.e., Kyrie, Gloria, Credo, Sanctus and Agnus Dei; a Latin text is used. The mass was commissioned by the Helsinki Alliance of Lutherans, and was premiered on 8 July 1963; the Finnish choral conductor Harald Andersén conducted the performance.

Figure 7.5 Row forms of *Missa a cappella*

Like many other multi-movement dodecaphonically styled works by Kokkonen, several row orderings serve as the basis for the pitch material in *Missa a cappella*. For instance, the Kyrie contains three different row orderings while the Agnus Dei contains five (the various row orderings are shown in Figure 7.5). Despite the mélange of harmonic resources, the progression illustrated in Figure 7.6 appears at the outset of the Kyrie and recurs numerous times untransposed in all five movements.

One interesting feature of the work is that it contains a greater number of tertian sonorities than other compositions from the same time period such as the 1962 *Sinfonia da camera* and 1964 *Opus Sonorum*—although, however, these triads are virtually always used as harmonic support for the dodecaphonic counterpoint. The two notable exceptions occur in the non-dodecaphonic structured Gloria and Credo: while these movements do not contain any tone rows, harmonic cohesion is generated through the repetition of a small number of motives that outline tertian sonorities. The Credo and Gloria are also more homophonic in texture when compared with the more contrapuntally oriented, dodecaphonically constructed Kyrie, Sanctus and Agnus Dei—a contrast no doubt due to the practical need to declaim the large amount of important text within these two movements. However, it should be noted that there is virtually no melismatic writing in any of the movements—a surprising feature of the Kyrie and Agnus Dei, movements in which the paucity of text conventionally renders the imitative contrapuntal lines more melismatic.

In many ways, the form of the five movements is quite traditional and articulated by changes in register, voices and texture. Consider, for instance, the design of the Kyrie, illustrated in Table 7.1. The movement is a ternary form, in accordance with the three lines of text; however, the three repetitions of each line of text are also cast in a ternary design.

Figure 7.6 *Missa a cappella*, Kyrie, mm. 1–2

Table 7.1 Formal design of *Missa a cappella*, Kyrie

Kyrie eleison

Section	Comments
Kyrie eleison (I)	Rows A, B, and a third contrapuntal line / three female voices.
Kyrie eleison (II)	Rows A, B, and a third contrapuntal line / three male voices.
Kyrie eleison (III)	Row A sung by the mezzo and alto; row B by the baritone.

Christie eleison

Section	Comments
Christie eleison (I)	Imitation between all the voices using rows A and C.
Christe eleison (II)	Homophonic passage using all the voices: row A by soprano.
Christie eleison (III)	Similar texture to opening of Christe eleison (I).

Kyrie eleison

Section	Comments
Kyrie eleison (I)	Rows A, B, and a third contrapuntal line / three male voices.
Kyrie eleison (II)	Primary harmonic progression involving all six voices.
Kyrie eleison (III)	Repetition of Kyrie eleison (II).

Laudatio Domini

Like the 1963 *Missa a cappella*, *Laudatio Domini* is a six-voice work written for soprano, mezzo-soprano, alto, tenor, baritone and bass. The piece was commissioned by the Finnish Radio Corporation in 1966 and premiered at the Camden Festival on 22 February, 1967; the important Finnish choral conductor Harald Andersén conducted the performance.

Although the *Laudatio Domini* has proven to be among Kokkonen's least known choral compositions, the work provides an early example of a perspective that increasingly dominated his later compositional style. Specifically, instead of using the various row orderings of a work in both the melodic and harmonic dimensions of a composition, a feature that appears in many of Kokkonen's works beginning from 1957, a significant percentage of the rows in *Laudatio Domini* are only used melodically (the row orderings of the five movements are shown in Figure 7.7). These melodies are not harmonized by other row elements but, rather, by tertian-styled triads. Further, as typically appears in Kokkonen's works, these tertian harmonies are associated melodically and not by functional syntax. However, approximately half of *Laudatio Domini* contains no dodecaphonic writing at all: instead, homophonic textures with tertian sonorities are used.

The Latin text for the five-movement work is taken from the Psalms of David—chronologically, verses from chapters 148, 29, 104, 90, and 104.

Figure 7.7 Row forms of *Laudatio Domini*

Erekhtheion

Kokkonen's solo cantata *Erekhtheion* was commissioned to commemorate the fiftieth anniversary of Turku University in 1970. The work was first performed on 28 February 1970 (the date is also the Finnish Day of Culture); the Finnish composer, conductor and musicologist Jouko Tolonen conducted the premiere. The Academy of Turku was home to the first university in Finland: the university was founded in 1640 and for approximately a century and a half Turku remained the intellectual center of Finland. However, the university was almost completely destroyed in the 1827 Great Fire of Turku and as a result it was transferred to Helsinki in 1828. For over ninety years the University of Helsinki (until 1919 the actual name of the university was the Imperial Alexander University of Finland) remained the sole university in Finland, until the founding of the University of Turku in 1920.

It seems to be somewhat of a tradition stemming back to Sibelius to mark festive occasions at Finnish universities with the performance of a new cantata. For instance, two noteworthy cantatas associated with the University of Turku that predate Kokkonen's *Erekhtheion* include Armas Järnefelt's (1869–1958) 1927 *Isänmann kasvot* (*The Face of the Fatherland*) and Tauno Pylkkänen's (1918–1980) *Soihdunkantajat* (*The Torch Bearers*) from 1955. The commission of *Erekhtheion* was the creation of the University of Turku's then rector Tauno Nurmela; he also commissioned the Finnish poet Arvi Nurmela to supply the text. The title of the work refers to the famous marble temple of the Acroplis in Athens designed by the Greek architect Mnesicles and built c. 420–405 B.C.

The work's four movements are quite different in character. For instance, the first, *Erekhtheion*, and (in particular) fourth and final movements, *This Land*, are inspirational in nature. In the first movement, for example, the opening text:

> Can Erekhtheion be born in Nordic lands,
> The sun temple to forest darkness?

is ultimately answered with:

> The unrestrained spring winds roll victorious over the sleeping land.

However, the most stirring lines are reserved for the end of the fourth movement, when the full chorus and soloists, supported by the entire orchestra, sing:

Thus over Finland burns in invitation
The great inextinguishable flame;
O People, follow the way of light uprightly
This country is an eternal gift to you.

By contrast, the third movement, *Dance of the Grown Men*, is light-hearted and humorous:

The flowing stripe of the dawn sun
Stands over the sleeping heath
And high up, in the air,
Men are dancing.
Happiness is in their feet,
When the heaviness of wandering years is long forgotten.

Erekhtheion is unusual on many counts. For instance, it is the least dissonant of any of Kokkonen's mature works: the vast majority of the harmonic language is derived from tonally-based triads that are virtually all related by root motion of a second or (more typically) a third; dissonances are treated primarily as passing motion. However, what makes the work really stand out in Kokkonen's oeuvre is its complete absence of tone rows. In fact, the one motive in the work that at all resembles a tone row ordering is the series of seven dyads shown in Figure 7.8. The series is actually only four distinct intervals as the latter three are a retrograde and inversion of the first three. Further, the series is realized with some freedom: at times all seven dyads appear in the order displayed; however, there are several instances when some of the dyads are reordered. Finally, while the series appears occasionally only as these dyads, they are frequently used in conjunction with an additional third pitch, generating major and minor triads, and it is these triads that serve as the basis for the majority of the harmonic material in the choral passages from the four movements.

Figure 7.8 Series of harmonic dyads in *Erekhtheion*

The series of dyads also has a role as the basis from which a large majority of the melodic material is generated. Consider, for instance, the repeating melodic figure sung by the baritone at the outset of the first movement: the eight-note melody proves to be an elaborated unfolding of the first three dyads of the harmonic series, indicating a further level of elaborative structure.

In sum, instead of a tone row, or a series of rows providing the primary pitch resource for a work, with tonal harmonies used in a supportive manner, an attribute of the majority of Kokkonen's post 1957 compositions, *Erekhtheion* is unusual in that elaboration and paraphrase of a restricted number of tonal harmonies or a short melodic fragment are the primary means by which Kokkonen forges a musical setting of the text. With such a limited harmonic palette, however, clearly other compositional parameters need to be employed to avoid monotony; texture proves to be of vital import in each movement. Consider, for instance, the stirring final movement, entitled *Tämä maa* (*This Land*). The form is a modified strophic design: each of the four stanzas of text are set the same way, with slight melodic changes in each stanza. The melody of each stanza is essentially harmonized with three harmonies, played by the strings—C Major, E Major and A♭ Major. While the pitch structure may not vary significantly between stanzas, there are alterations to each stanza that, in the end, generate the movement's crescendo design: not only is there a different vocal timbre (baritone, stanza one; soprano, stanza two; chorus, stanza three; soloists and chorus, stanza four), but also an increase in the number of instruments used with successive stanzas. For instance, in stanza one, the baritone is supported by *pizzicato* violas and cellos and short motivic fragments by the flutes, oboes and trumpets; by stanza four the entire orchestra, including the bass drum, cymbal and tympani is deployed, ending the movement (and the work) triumphantly with the text "O People, follow the way of light uprightly; This country is an eternal gift to you."

As a final note, there are several names referred to in the third movement which were associated with Turku University; as such, the inclusion of their names represents an act of homage to the university. Aleksi Käpy and Uno Ludvig Lehtonen were president and a high ranking official, respectively, of the University Society; Kaarlo Jäntere, Uno Harva, T. M. Kivimäki and J. E. Salomaa were professors; and K. N. Rantakari was chancellor.

Sub rosa

The song cycle *Sub rosa* for mezzo soprano and piano was written between 1972 and 1973. The texts are a series of four poems by the Finnish modernist poet Eeva-Liisa Manner (1921–1995). The four songs marked

Allegretto moderato, Molto tranquillo, Allegro ma non troppo and *Moderato* follow one another without pause. The work was premiered on 18 March 1973 by the Finnish mezzo soprano Heljä Angervo and the celebrated Japanese-born pianist Izumi Tateno.

The five tone rows (from two different row orderings) illustrated in Figure 7.9 generate a significant percentage of the composition's pitch material: row B is an inversional form of row A; row C is a slightly modified version of row A; and rows D and E are inversionally related to each other (these latter two rows only appear in the second song).

Figure 7.9 Row forms of *Sub rosa*

While the five rows generate a vital amount of the pitch material for both the vocalist and pianist, there are two additional pitch resources for the piano part. The first is to combine a series of perfect 5th intervals in the left hand with various realizations of the tones rows played by the right hand, thus generating tertian sonorities by the arrangement. A second pitch resource is to simply harmonize elements of a tone row with tertian sonorities—a strategy used, of course, in many of Kokkonen's works.

Requiem

The origins of Kokkonen's Requiem date from around 1978. With the resounding success of *The Last Temptations*, the Finnish conductor Ulf Söderblom was eager to commission from Kokkonen a large-scale work that employed a chorus. Söderblom used his choral group Akateeminen Laulu to commission a relatively non-descript "large-scale work for chorus and orchestra." Not long after receiving the commission, however, Kokkonen's second wife Maija died from cancer. The nature of the composition took on a different meaning for him, and he used the opportunity to compose a requiem mass in her memory. The work took two years to complete, an unusual length of time for Kokkonen, and can no doubt be largely attributed to the emotional turmoil he experienced after losing his spouse of over twenty-five years. The work received its premiere on 17 September 1981, with Söderblom conducting the performance: it was immediately hailed a masterpiece and is widely considered to be the greatest of all Finnish requiem masses.

The Requiem is cast in nine movements. The work differs in several respects from such celebrated masses by Berlioz, Mozart and Verdi—absent, for instance, is the austerity of the opening Requiem aeternum movement from Berlioz's mass and the fear and terror of the Dies irae from Mozart's and Verdi's Requiems is absent. Rather, Kokkonen's Requiem is more gentle and peaceful than these other famous masses—in fact, it is among the most optimistic in spirit from the canon of requiem masses. Given that the composition was written for the memory of his wife, it is not implausible to suggest a programmatic message behind the choice (and absence) of particular texts and the nature of the musical setting: namely, that Kokkonen believed there was comfort in death and that Maija had nothing to fear in the afterlife. As a consequence, any texts that suggested such apprehension were redundant.

The pitch material of the Requiem is derived from a collage of techniques that typify Kokkonen's later works. For instance, the Kyrie is constructed almost entirely from twelve-tone rows and any harmonies are generated from the interaction between these various rows. By contrast, the Agnus Dei contains no tone rows whatsoever and its pitch material is almost all derived from tonal progressions that are non-functional in nature. The majority of the movements, however, combine these two harmonic resources.

One interesting aspect of the Requiem is the pervasive appearance of an E Major triad. Not only does the triad feature prominently in the piece, but it also appears as the final sonority in six of the nine movements—in fact, there is symmetrical design to the work: movements one, two, three and seven, eight and nine all end with the triad. By means of contrast, however, the middle three movements end with an A♭ Major, B minor (with an added C♯) and A Major, respectively (note, however, that the three harmonies all contain invariant pitches with E Major).

Requiem aeternam

The works opens with two motives that prove vital throughout the opening movement: (1) a Major 2nd dyad, which through a sustained dynamic crescendo is altered via contrary motion to a Major 3rd (as we shall come to see, this motive is also significant in other movements); and (2) a descending minor 2nd, used as a musical symbol of lament. The movement, marked *Andante*, is a bipartite design: each part begins with the minor 2nd/ Major 3rd motive followed by a statement of the text "Requiem aeternam dona eis, Domine, et lux perpetua luceat eis" ("Grant them eternal rest, O Lord, And may perpetual light shine upon them"); the third statement of this text forms the basis for the coda. The appearance of the soloists represents a further distinguishing feature between the two large parts: the baritone is used in part one and the soprano for part two; the soprano is also used for the short coda.

Parts one and two may be each subdivided into five similar sections. Section one contains the Major 2nd/Major 3rd motive. An expanded elaboration of the descending minor 2nd motive forms the basis of the pitch material in section two; compared with section one, the texture is enlarged through the addition of four-voice homophony by the chorus. A significant portion of section three develops the opening Major 2nd/Major 3rd motive, now transposed to the pitches B/C♯ – B♭/D; neighbor notes elaborate the motive. In section four a greater number of neighbor and passing notes elaborate the B/C♯ – B♭/D motive; of note are the extensive octave/unison lines that utilize all four vocal parts. Section five contains numerous repetitions of a syllabic setting of the text "Deus in Sion"; A Major triads and G minor 7th sonorities feature prominently. While there is no comparable section in part two, the syllabic setting of the text "Requiem aeternum," again using numerous A Major and G minor 7th chords, suggests an elision between the end of part two and the coda.

In the coda, statements of the text "Requiem aeternum" are once again accompanied by the minor 2nd/Major 3rd motive. However, the motive is transposed to oscillate between F/G and E/G♯, a strategy that allows for an E Major triad to end the movement.

Kyrie

All of the pitch material for the soloists, chorus and orchestra of the Kyrie is constructed from the two twelve-tone rows illustrated in Figure 7.10. In general, row A is associated with the "Kyrie eleison" text and row B for the "Christie eleison" text. The use of the rows is fairly segregated between these texts, although in mm. 150–156 both appear simultaneously during a dialogue between the two soloists: row A is realized by the baritone soloist; the soprano realizes row B (the orchestral accompaniment is virtually all generated from row A). As in the Requiem aeternum, the movement ends with an E Major triad, although now at a dynamic level of triple *forte*.

Figure 7.10 Row forms of Requiem, Kyrie

Tractus

The Tractus is, like the Kyrie, primarily constructed from twelve-tone procedures. Only the row ordering shown in Figure 7.11 is used, although several different row forms are employed; P_3 (the row displayed) and I_{10} (B♭,C,B,A,A♭,F,F♯,E,E♭,C♯,D,G) are the most common.

Figure 7.11 Row form of Requiem, Tractus

The movement opens at an *andante* tempo with realizations of P_3, imitated by the soprano, alto and bass to the words "absolve Domine"; the orchestral accompaniment is primarily based on realizations of the I_{10} row form. The basses entrance in m. 196 is derived by I_1 and establishes a new section commencing in m. 202, one based upon I row forms, although the orchestral accompaniment still engages P row forms (the text employed in this section is "Animas omnium fidelium defunctorum ab omni vinculo delictorum").

The return to the initial text, "absolve Domine," contains a concomitant arrival of the opening imitative idea; however, three different rows are now utilized: P_3 by the soprano and alto, P_4 by the bass, and I_{10} by the tenor. By m. 226, the voices coalesce into a three-chord ostinato; it ends with the B♭ Major harmony in m. 242, and is immediately followed by the first of the movement's two dramatic gestures: an a cappella octave/unison statement of a descending Major 7th interval. Figure 7.12 illustrates the three chord ostinato beginning from m. 232 and ends with the descending Major 7th gesture in m. 250–253.

A short, violent orchestral interlude follows the second a cappella statement in mm. 285–288; the pitch material is derived from P$_1$. Following the interlude, the remainder of the movement is calm and serene; the text "Et lucis aeternae beatitudine perfrui" ("And may they be refreshed by the glory of the eternal light") is used for this final section. I$_{11}$ is the row form from which the pitch material for the final section is based—and more accurately, for the soprano, as the lower three voices form tertian-based triads as harmonic support for the successive elements of the row. The Tractus ends quietly, once again with an E Major triad.

Figure 7.12 Requiem, mm. 235–253 (piano/vocal reduction)

Figure 7.12, continued

Domine Jesu Christe

A large percentage of the harmonic and melodic material in Domine Jesu Christe is derived from the series of five harmonic dyads presented at the opening of the movement (shown in Figure 7.13).

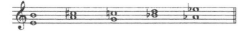

Figure 7.13 Series of dyads in Requiem, Domine Jesu Christe

Unlike the first three movements, the majority of the harmonies in Domine Jesu Christe are tertian-based triads and, specifically, those derived from the opening dyad series, i.e., E, A, C, B♭ and A♭ (both Major and minor triads are possible). However, the numerous repetitions of the dyad series generate greater harmonic redundancy when compared with the prior three movements. A corollary to this last point is that a significant percentage of the melodic material from the choral parts is either an element from the five triads of the series or a neighbor, or passing, note to an element of these triads.

Domine Jesu Christe is a ternary design. Part A contains numerous statements of the dyad series by the orchestra as well as the chorus. The soprano soloist is featured: the basis of the soprano's pitch material is the upper or lower elements from the series of five dyads; elaborations of this five-pitch melody, however, are frequent.

Part B begins at m. 359 and is characterized by an alternation between the baritone soloist and chorus (the baritone's first entrance began near the end of part A at m. 350 where it doubled the soprano's line one octave below). A distinguishing feature of this part of the movement is the pervasive semitonal neighbor-note figure played by the accompanying strings. Part B culminates with the E Major chord at m. 382; a short transition for orchestra and chorus leads to part A' beginning at m. 389, a modified version of the opening of the movement.

Like the opening, the soprano's melodic lines in part A' are harmonically supported by the chorus. However, an important difference is that the dyads from the harmonic series are now frequently superimposed upon each other. For instance, between mm. 397 and 407 the dyad combinations of B/E and A/C♯ and (only briefly) G/C and B♭/D are used (the extended duration of these dyad combinations beautifully captures the text, "eas in lucem sanctam" ("bring them into eternal light")). The movement ends with the word "sanctum" on a sustained A♭ Major chord, i.e., the final dyad of the harmonic series.

Hostias et Preces

The Hostias et Preces movement is set in a lilting, dance-like manner. The constant metric shift between $\frac{6}{8}$ and $\frac{2}{4}$ as well as several melodic gestures strongly recall the dance hall scene of act one – scene two from *The Last Temptations*. As the central movement of the work, it is unique on at least two counts: (1) it is the shortest in duration of the nine movements; and (2) it is the only movement that does not end with a major triad but, rather, with the tetrachord {B,C♯,D,F♯}, along with a bass note pedal A.

The movement is a bipartite form; each part is itself divided into two sections. Section one (m. 441 for part one; m. 468 for part two) is characterized by numerous different tertian sonorities, along with neighbor-note figures associated with virtually each harmony; successive chords in a progression are related to each other either by neighbor chords or invariant pitch relationships from chord relationships of a Major or minor 3rd. The long-range harmonic strategy is elusive; however, the goal of section one in both parts is A Major. By contrast, the harmonic rhythm in section two is much slower than the first section (in part one, section two begins at m. 448; in part two, at m. 484). As an illustration, consider the opening harmony of part one/section two, {B,C♯,D,F♯}, employed from mm. 448 until 455. Only this tetrachord is heard during these eight measures; the neighbor-notes from the vocal lines do not generate new harmonies but, rather, forge voice exchanges between various harmonic elements of the tetrachord. However, like section one, any real harmonic changes are forged via minimal voice-leading between adjacent voices—for instance, the {B,C♯,D,F♯} harmony from mm. 448–455 noted earlier is converted to {C,D,E,F♯} in m. 456 and {C,E,F,G} in m. 458.

Sanctus

The Sanctus opens with great rhythmic vitality and drive. Syncopated statements of the pentachord {C♯,F♯,B,E,A} (derived from an incomplete interval-5 cycle) punctuate string ostinatos, as well as a repeating six-note motive played by the oboe; both are also derived from the same interval-5 cycle pentachord (Figure 7.14 illustrates a representative passage from mm. 497–500). The various ostinatos complement thirteen repetitions of the word "Sanctus." A T_1 transposition of the pentachord in m. 511 {D,G,C,F,B♭} demarcates the change in text to "Domine Deus"; the section ends with a two-measure *fortissimo* statement of an A♭ triad on the word "Sabaoth."

Section two of the movement begins at m. 515. The two string ostinatos based on the opening pentachord {A (bass note),B,C♯,D,F♯} return and now harmonize eighteen repetitions of the word "Sanctus." New, however, are the two rows realized numerous times as melodic gestures by both the orchestra and soprano soloist. Figure 7.15 illustrates the T_5 relationship between the first six order positions of the two row forms.

Figure 7.14 Requiem, mm. 497–500 (piano/vocal reduction)

Figure 7.15 Row forms of Requiem, Sanctus

At m. 534 there is a reduction in orchestral texture and rhythmic activity, as well as a shift from the interval-5 based harmonies that characterized the opening sections to one where tertian triads become the harmonic material of interest. Intervals of seconds and thirds feature prominently between successive harmonies. The soprano soloist is the only voice used in this new section (the chorus is silent); the two tone rows introduced in the prior section continue to be used.

Section four begins at m. 551 and retains the pitch and harmonic features from the prior section; however, the soloists are now absent and the texture is comprised of a divisi chorus and orchestra. The section ends with the text "Hosanna in excelsis," and a cadence on a D Major triad, played *fortissimo*.

Measures 573–580 contain a brief orchestral interlude between the Sanctus and Benedictus in which the pitch material is largely generated from the two row forms. The Benedictus proper begins in m. 581 with a harmonic focus thus far not heard—B♭. The section is dominated by the baritone soloist. However, the soloist's melodic material is not obtained from realizations of the nine-note rows from the Sanctus, but rather from pitches of the underlying harmonic progression in which tertian sonorities play a significant role. The movement ends with a prolonged focus upon A Major played *fortissimo* (the passage is scored for the entire orchestra, both soloists and chorus).

Agnus Dei

The Agnus Dei is, appropriately given the tripartite-styled text, designed in three sections: section I (mm. 624–644) is for chorus and orchestra; section II (mm. 645–660) for soprano soloist, chorus and orchestra; and section III (mm. 661–685) is for baritone soloist, chorus and orchestra. The movement opens with the same gesture and orchestration as the opening Requiem aeternum movement, namely a Major 2nd interval which expands into a Major 3rd interval via contrary motion. However, the motive is now transposed up a minor 3rd, i.e., from F/G to E/G♯, suggesting a progression to E Major—not only the most prevalent triad in the movement, but also the final goal harmony in each of the three sections (in fact, the final twelve measures of the movement are nothing but a prolongation of an E Major triad).

There are no dodecaphonic procedures employed in the Agnus Dei. Rather, there is a preponderance of neighboring chords as well as a concomitant number of repeating neighbor and passing melodic figures that permeate the movement, emphasizing the central E Major tonality. Figure 7.16 illustrates a representative passage, as regards melodic activity and E Major centricity, in mm. 659–668 (i.e., the final two measures of section II and opening measures of section III).

Figure 7.16 Requiem, mm. 659–668 (piano/vocal reduction)

In Paradisum

In Paradisum introduces an interesting new texture to the work: the soloists and chorus all sing identical parts at the octave/unison throughout the movement. There are no tone rows; rather, the text is set by two categories of melodic motives—specifically, <A-F♯-E-F-G-A♭> (hexachord A) and <E-F♯-A-G-A♭-B♭> (hexachord B). There are eight phrases: each, with the exception of the fourth, an orchestral interlude, is a melodic elaboration of one of the two hexachords. Further, the symmetrical pattern to the ordering of these hexachords generates the movement's binary design, shown in Table 7.2.

Like the prior Agnus Dei, In Paradisum ends peacefully with an E Major triad.

Table 7.2 Formal Design of In Paradisum from Requiem

Hexachord		Measure no.
A		686
B		689
B		696
C	(orchestral interlude)	701
A		709
B		713
B		719
A		725

Lux aeterna

The final movement Lux aeterna, like the Requiem aeternum and Agnus Dei, begins with a Major 2nd interval played by the strings that expands outward via contrary melodic motion; in particular, the similarity between the opening Requiem aeternum movement, as regards dynamic level and orchestration, suggests a type of recapitulation with the opening of the work. However, while the motive earlier had expanded from a Major 2nd to a Major 3rd and was primarily restricted to the low strings, in the present movement it enlarges to either a perfect 4th or perfect 5th and, aside from the opening measures, is placed in an upper register and associated with the woodwinds. In addition, the melodic expansion and contraction is not just cast in long rhythmic values but in a variety of rhythmic settings, including trill-like figures.

Lux aeterna is a binary-form design in accordance with the two-part design of text: both parts begins with the expansion from a Major 2nd to a perfect $4^{th}/5^{th}$, followed by an extensive passage for a soloist supported harmonically by the chorus (the soprano, alto and tenor parts are consistently scored divisi) and orchestra; the baritone is the soloist for part one and the soprano for part two. The pitch material for the soloists is realized from the twelve-tone row shown in Figure 7.17. By contrast, however, the pitch material of the chorus and orchestra is primarily derived from incomplete interval-5 cycle pentachords—for example, {C♯,F♯,B,E,A}.

Two E Major chords bring Lux aeterna, and the Requiem, to a peaceful conclusion: the first triad is played by the strings and woodwinds, the second by the chorus alone singing the word "lux."

Figure 7.17 Row form of Requiem, Lux aeterna

Note

1. The Wihuri Foundation Award was established in 1942 by Antti and Jenny Wihuri. Since the inception, the purpose of the annual scholarship has been to promote cultural endeavors throughout financial grants and prizes. Other notable recipients of the award have included Sibelius, Eric Bergman, Usko Meriläinen and Einojuhani Rautavaara.

Chapter 8

Chamber Works

Piano Trio

The Piano Trio was written in 1948 and can be justifiably labeled Kokkonen's opus 1. It is certainly the most substantive work he had written up to that point in his career—the prior decade consisted of only short piano works and miscellaneous songs—and the advance the trio represented over these earlier works, as regards pitch construction and formal design, undoubtedly allowed Kokkonen to enlarge his compositional thinking, a process of growth which led to the Piano Quintet a few years later, the composition widely considered to be the first major work from his oeuvre.

The trio is one of the most formally unambiguous and harmonically clear-cut works in Kokkonen's oeuvre; along with the Piano Quintet, it displays the most extensive influence from his early attraction to Hindemith's music. The close relationships shared by the sonata form themes demonstrate a further attribute in many of Kokkonen's early compositions—specifically, his interest in mono-thematic formal designs.

The trio was premiered on 12 October 1948 by Heikki Louhivuori, violin, Seppo Laamanen, cello, and Kokkonen on piano, at a music festival held at Aula University in Oslo, Norway.

Movement One

The first movement is a sonata-form design. It opens with a brief, *adagio* introduction in which the primary motivic material from the exposition is presented. The exposition proper begins at m. 14. The vigorous first theme is shown in Figure 8.1 (two motives of import, X and Y, are indicated in the figure). A transition based upon motive X begins at m. 24, leading to the second theme at m. 42; the theme is an elaborated version of theme one.

The development begins at m. 61; the highlight is the gradual accumulation of motive Y from theme one, leading to its culmination, both in registral expanse and dynamic level, in mm. 95–101. The recapitulation begins at m. 123 and aside from the abridged transition, is rather nondescript—although given the rather assertive centricity towards E♭

Major throughout the movement, the focus upon G during the final measures is rather surprising.

Figure 8.1 Piano Trio, mov. 1, mm. 14–23

Movement Two

The second movement, marked *Andante tranquillo e semplice*, is a rondo; the tempo marking may be a reference to the uncomplicated quality of the predominantly modal harmonic language, the nearly relentless quarter-note pulse running throughout the movement, and the straightforward formal design. The refrain is essentially two lines of invertible counterpoint (the refrain appears at m. 1, m. 17, m. 25, m. 42 and m. 64). A chord progression played by the solo piano follows the two-voice counterpoint and functions as a type of cadence; a feature of the movement's structure is the gradual melodic elaboration of the progression with each successive appearance.

An episode appears at three different points in the movement—at m. 11, m. 33 and m. 57. While the first and third appearances are A-Dorian in flavor, the second, and most extensive, appearance contains a shift to A Major; the latter episode also represents the moment in the design when the textural density increases, leading to the culmination when all three instruments contribute simultaneously to the refrain.

Figure 8.2 Piano Trio, mov. 3, mm. 1–12

Movement Three

The final movement is a seven-part rondo set at a brisk tempo; the refrain is itself a five-part rondo design (i.e., a–b–a–b–a). The opening two sections of the refrain (i.e., sections a and b) in mm. 1–12 are shown in Figure 8.2; of note is the E♭ tonal focus for the a section and the lower neighbor D for section b (the last system in the figure), a feature that appears throughout.

    The first episode begins at m. 43 and consists of the imitative dialogue between the two string instruments, accompanied by the piano. The second episode begins at m. 149 following the first reprise of the refrain (mm. 89–141) and short transition in mm. 142–148 (aside from its different orchestration, the material and form of the second refrain remains the same as the first). It is essentially a uni-directional increase in register, texture and dynamic level upon a succession of transpositions of a simple melodic gesture beginning in C minor. Following a somewhat extended transition based upon motives from the second episode (the transition lasts from mm. 184–213), two further appearances of an abridged version of the refrain emerge at m. 214 and m. 292 (the refrain here is only a three-part structure, i.e., a–b–a). A third episode appears at m. 246 and is virtually identical to the first. A rousing coda begins at m. 336 and features motivic material from the second episode.

Piano Quintet

The 1953 Piano Quintet ranks as among the most significant of Kokkonen's pre-dodecaphonic works, one that warrants a place alongside the other chamber pieces from Kokkonen's mature period. The quintet is the most formally secure of Kokkonen's early works and has consistently received praise as the *sine qua non* exemplar of Kokkonen's particular approach to neoclassicism. It is also the composition to which one typically refers when influences such as Bartók, Hindemith (in particular) and Shostakovich upon Kokkonen's early style are discussed.

    The four-movement work was composed between 1951 and 1953 and was premiered on 26 October 1953 in Helsinki in the first concert completely devoted to Kokkonen's music; the composer was the pianist for the performance.

Movement One

The first movement is a sonata-form design without a development section, followed by a coda. Figure 8.3 illustrates the two thematic ideas from theme group one in mm. 1–7 and 11–17; interval-class 5 plays a vital role in both themes. Theme I/B—in effect three phrases—appears twice: in mm. 11–34 the theme is stated by the piano with support of theme I/A by the strings; and in mm. 36–56 the first violin plays theme I/B with support of theme I/A by the piano.

A transition to theme two begins at m. 65; a series of harmonic dyads underscores the transition's prominent descending chromatic line. While the interval series is retained in theme two, it is distinguished by a change in tempo (*poco piu mosso*) and its aggressive rhythmic profile. Initially the theme is played by only the first violin; by m. 91, all four strings play a unison/octave version of it.

A reduction in tempo at m. 107 initiates the closing theme group; two thematic ideas are used. The first is based upon a chromatic line passed between the strings; the second theme is a triplet figure played by the piano (the latter is a variant of theme I/A from theme group one).

The recapitulation begins at m. 135. It opens with a variant of theme I/A, imitated between the various instruments; the imitation ultimately leads to the theme's octave/unison realization at m. 162, a statement that immediately segues to an interesting passage between mm. 167 and 202 which contains extensive development of theme I/B. The series of harmonic dyads and aggressive theme that distinguished theme two reappears at m. 203, albeit briefly (five measures in duration). The brevity of the section, however, is compensated by the rather expansive closing theme group.

The grand pause at m. 244 announces the coda; it contains three sections. In section one, the three phrases of the exposition's version of theme I/B are played by the cello; sustained harmonies by the remaining strings and a melodic ostinato by the piano support the cello's melody. In section two (mm. 261–265), theme I/A from the exposition returns, played by the solo piano; and in section three all the instruments articulate continuously the first six pitches of theme I/B. The movement ends calmly on an open 5th interval D-A.

Figure 8.3 Piano Quintet, mov. 1, mm. 1–20

Movement Two

The second movement scherzo is a ternary form. The bipartite-designed part A, marked *Allegro*, opens with a vigorous theme played by the strings; interval-class 5 features prominently in the theme.

A transition to the b section, scored entirely for the piano, begins at m. 22. The section proper begins at m. 30: a new theme appears and is stated three times (at m. 30, m. 34 and m. 38: the first and third statements are identical; the middle statement, however, is a T_5 transposition of the outer two). All three statements are performed by the first violin; the remaining strings and piano function as harmonic support.

An a' section begins at m. 46 with three statements of its theme: the first statement at m. 46 is for the piano alone; the second begins at m. 51 for the first violin with harmonic support by the three other strings; and the third statement, beginning at m. 56, is again by piano, this time with support by all four strings. The b section returns at m. 62. As before, the section contains three statements of the theme—however, all three statements are now played by the piano with harmonic support by the four strings. Despite the similarities between the two b sections, however, an important distinction is that the dynamic level in the second b section increases to a much greater degree over the initial *fortissimo*. Part A ends with a series of repetitions of an A Major triad.

Part B, marked *Poco piu lento*, begins at m. 95; it is cast in a ternary design. Section a, for strings alone, contains a harmonic ostinato played by the second violin and viola that suggests a G♯ minor tonal focus. The thematic material is based upon four phrases: phrases one and three are played by the first violin; phrases two and four by the cello. The piano is the focus of the brief b section, which plays a melodic figure reminiscent of the primary theme of the a section from Part A. The a section returns at m. 118: as before, the tonal focus is G♯ minor, although now the harmonic ostinato is shared among the different instruments.

Part A' begins at m. 141. The thematic material from the earlier part A returns, as well as the interaction between the first violin and piano in the realization of the various thematic statements; a notable addition is the Alberti-bass styled left-hand accompaniment by the piano, engendering greater rhythmic energy to the passage.

A short coda begins at m. 210 and contains the harmonic ostinato and thematic material from part B. However, the theme is abruptly cut off, and the movement ends with a two-measure flourish of the opening thematic idea, played by all the instruments at a *fortissimo* dynamic level.

Movement Three

The *Adagio* third movement is a simple rondo design. The first two (of four) phrases from the refrain are illustrated in Figure 8.4 (the first three phrases are played by the first violin; the fourth is played by the second

violin; subsequent appearances of the refrain appear at m. 40, m. 85 and m.
121). Of note is the dotted eighth/sixteenth-note figure, a rhythmic motive
that is featured in every appearance of the refrain as well as the coda.

Figure 8.4 Piano Quintet, mov. 3, mm. 1–13

The one episode appears at m. 25, m. 51 and m. 112 (the latter two
appearances are elaborated versions of the first). Like the refrain, its initial
appearance is scored for only the strings and contains a harmonic
accompaniment whose rhythm is predominantly in half-notes.

Measure 40 marks the return of the refrain and the piano's first
appearance in the movement. Only two phrases of the theme are used; both
are played by the cello and supported by left-hand dyads from the low
register of the piano. A slightly varied version of the episode's theme
returns at m. 51. In essence, all five instruments state the theme in

succession (the sole exception is the entry by the first violin, which affirms a version of the first episode's theme): with each statement, the density of texture and dynamic level increase, leading to the fifth entry (by the piano) where all the instruments are utilized.

Movement Four

The final movement, marked *Allegro moderato*, is a sonata-form design. Theme one consists of a series of inversionally related imitative ideas; as with many of the themes from the earlier movements, interval-class 5 represents an important motivic element. With each subsequent entry, the overall texture increases so that by the fifth, all the instruments contribute.

A transition to theme two begins at m. 17; the repeating chromatic D-D♯-E baseline anticipates the E-D-D♯ ostinato that pervades theme two. Theme two, beginning at m. 22, consists of four related phrases: three are played by the cello; the fourth is a unison statement by the two violins. The capricious styled closing theme is repeated twice, and each time with slight variation: the first two statements feature the piano; the first violin is used for the third.

The development section begins at m. 59. A significant portion of it consists of a piano ostinato that is a rhythmic diminution of theme two; the ostinato supports melodic material stated by the two violins (in unison) of a rhythmically augmented version of theme one.

The recapitulation begins at m. 88. Interestingly, the order of the three themes is reversed: the closing theme appears first at m. 88; the four-phrases from theme two appear at m. 103; and theme one begins at m. 118.

A coda begins at m. 176. The section contains numerous statements of theme one's thematic ideas, albeit at a much lower dynamic level. The movement ends with a stirring three-measure octave/unison outburst of the opening portion of theme one played at a *fortissimo* dynamic level.

Duo for Violin and Piano

The *Duo* was written in 1955 for the Finnish violinist Pauvo Rautio and pianist Timo Mäkinen. The two performers, along with the cellist Matti Rautio (the brother of Pauvo), were members of an ensemble that toured extensively within Finland and abroad during the 1950s and 1960s. Mäkinen, a close personal friend of Kokkonen, was also a musicologist of note. Rautio and Mäkinen premiered the *Duo* on 6 November 1955 at the Sibelius Academy, in Helsinki.

While the formal design and melodic and harmonic structures of the *Duo* are such that it may be classified as one of the composer's neoclassical works, what makes the *Duo* a point of departure in Kokkonen's oeuvre is its decreased reliance upon tertian sonorities to articulate form, when compared with earlier works such as the Piano Trio or Piano Quintet. Instead, a much greater percentage of the melodic and harmonic dimensions in the *Duo* is generated via intervallic associations—in particular, interval-class 5. For instance, Figure 8.5 illustrates the extensive use of interval-class 5 to generate the opening segment of the first theme from movement one. While the work is not a twelve-tone composition, the use of chromatic aggregates to structure many of the themes and harmonies, along the numerous successive repetitions of these themes makes the *Duo* a valuable work to study, as regards Kokkonen's compositional evolution to the 1957 *Music for String Orchestra*, his first composition to use tone rows per se to generate the harmonic structure in a work.

Movement One

The *Allegro* first movement is a sonata-form design. The first theme is stated four times: the first and last statements are by the solo piano; the second and third by the violin. In addition to the changes in orchestration, variety is generated by the alterations to the registral position of the thematic statements as well as the accompanimental figures by the piano. Theme two begins at m. 46: it is based upon an eight-note motive and is essentially a decorated version of the B-F♯-F-B♭ motive that initiates theme one (see, in particular, the violin and piano right-hand motives). Another eight-note motive generates the closing theme beginning at m. 79. Like the first and second themes, interval-class 5 is central to its structure.

The development begins at m. 95. All the themes from the exposition are manipulated: the closing theme is featured at m. 95; theme one at m. 111; and theme 2 at m. 130. A transition at m. 184 leads to the recapitulation at m. 198. There are two notable alterations from the exposition: (1) the absence of the solo piano version of theme one; and (2) the closing theme (at m. 230) is now used as a transition between theme one and theme two (theme two begins at m. 249). A coda derived from theme one begins at m. 265 and brings the movement to end calmly on a B♭-F dyad.

Figure 8.5 *Duo*, mov. 1, mm. 1–7

Movement Two

The charming second movement, an intermezzo marked *Allegro grazioso*, is also a sonata-form design. Theme one is stated three successive times—the first two by the violin, the third by the piano (the first statement is shown in Figure 8.6).

A transition comprised of motivic material from theme one begins at m. 31; the final measures of the transition contain a piano ostinato that serves as the primary harmonic support for theme two. Of note is that theme two is a rhythmically altered version of the right-hand motivic material from theme one.

The development begins at m. 111. The first section contains the first theme, only an octave higher than in the exposition. The piano ostinato that formed the basis of theme two appears at m. 142, signaling the beginning of a new section. However, the theme is almost immediately abandoned to further develop theme one—for instance, at m. 148 theme one appears in a rhythmically diminuted and elaborated version. Following an extended period of focus on this elaborated version of theme one, theme two appears briefly in the piano at m. 231 and is used as transitional material for the relatively nondescript recapitulation.

Figure 8.6 *Duo*, mov. 2, mm. 1–10

Movement Three

Like the prior two movements, the final movement is a sonata-from design—although it is the only one of the three to begin with an *adagio* introduction. A spirited first theme from the exposition begins at m. 40; it is characterized by a prominent dotted-eighth note rhythm and an accompanimental pattern whose pitch structure utilizes the octatonic collection $OCT_{0,1}$ to a large degree.

The second theme begins at m. 75. The B-F♯-B♭-F motive that played a vital role in the first movement is of significance here. The accompaniment is based upon two harmonic resources: a series of four arpeggiated triads (D Major, B♭ Major, G minor and E minor) and the octatonic collection $OCT_{0,1}$.

The development begins at m. 103; it is comprised of three sections preceded by an introductory passage. Section one contains a piano ostinato that supports development of theme one. In section two (beginning at m. 131) the series of harmonic dyads that featured prominently in the introduction is extensively developed with support by the piano using two harmonic resources: (1) the harmonic accompaniment from theme one; and (2) the scalar realization of the octatonic collection $OCT_{0,1}$ utilized in theme two. Section three (beginning at m. 141) contains imitation of the opening motive from theme one between the two instruments.

An abridged recapitulation begins at m. 173. Of note is the substantial alteration to theme two: it appears for only four measures and is quickly abandoned to return to theme one. As a means of contrast with the abridged recapitulation, there is a lengthy coda beginning at m. 210, in which both themes are further examined. The work ends with a rousing series of cadential gestures whose focus is an A triad.

String Quartet No. 1

Although Kokkonen began work on both the first string quartet and Symphony No. 1 during the spring of 1958, the quartet was completed first, in February of 1959; it was premiered on 5 March 1959 in Helsinki by the Helsinki Quartet. Immediately remarkable is the considerable advance in dodecaphonic construction that the quartet and symphony display over the serial procedures in the song cycle *Hades of the Birds* and *Music for String Orchestra* from a couple of years earlier and, in particular, the sophisticated interaction of harmonic materials that the various twelve-tone row forms generate, both within and between movements, harmonic associations that anticipate Kokkonen's mature twelve-tone works.

Movement One

The pitch material of the first movement, marked *Allegro*, is based upon the three rows shown in Figure 8.7. Row A is the most prevalent (row I/B is the inverted form of row I/A beginning on the same pitch, B). The movement is a sonata form in which the harmonic contrast between these three rows generates the formal design in a manner analogous with the use of tonal argument in a traditional sonata.

The sonata is preceded by a fifty-six measure introduction. Row I/A dominates and is realized: (1) as partitioned between the four instruments (the opening measures); (2) as played by a single instrument (in mm. 16–17 both the viola and cello play a realization of the row); and (3) as a harmonic sonority employing some, or, at times, all of the four instruments. Although row I/B occasionally appears, it is used by either the viola or cello in a descending contour, as opposed to an ascending line by the violins.

The exposition proper begins at m. 57. The aggressive first theme, played by the first violin in its characteristic contour and rhythmic profile, is shown in Figure 8.8. By m. 80 the energy and dynamic level begin to diminish and at m. 90 theme two appears: the contrasting theme is cast at a lower dynamic level and utilizes longer rhythmic values when compared with the first theme. Importantly, it is generated from a new harmonic resource, row I/C, accompanied by harmonic dyads obtained from row A (played *pizzicato* by the viola and cello). A closing theme based on a rhythmic figure of triplet-eighth notes and generated from row I/A begins at m. 126; ostinatos represent an important distinguishing feature.

Figure 8.7 Row forms of String Quartet No. 1, mov. 1

Figure 8.8 String Quartet No. 1, mov. 1, mm. 57–70

The development begins at m. 159; it contains extensive manipulation of the rhythmic figures that characterize the three thematic ideas of the exposition. An abridged recapitulation begins at m. 252. Theme two contains an interesting change (the theme begins at m. 277): while the rhythmic values of the pitches in the recapitulation are, like the exposition, fairly long in duration, the meter remains consistently $\frac{3}{4}$ (in the exposition it oscillated between $\frac{2}{4}$ and $\frac{3}{4}$). The closing theme begins at m. 287 and elides with the second theme, which does not actually end until m. 296. The movement ends quietly with a sonority garnered from the first eight pitches of row I/A.

Movement Two

The dodecaphonic procedures employed in the second movement are significantly more complex than the first. Four different six-element rows are used (these are seen in Figure 8.9): rows II/A and II/B are inversionally related to each other; row II/D is a T_7 transposition of row II/C (the latter two rows are based upon a different row ordering than rows II/A and II/B). A comparison between rows II/A and II/B and rows I/A and I/B from movement one is insightful. Specifically, the interval classes between order positions 1 and 2 and order positions 3 and 4 are the same, a feature that Kokkonen exploits by frequently slurring these order positions together, thereby prompting a subtle aural similarity between the two movements. However, the dramatic difference between the remaining intervals of the two rows ultimately forges the more overt harmonic distinction between the two pairs of rows (and, therefore, between the movements).

The movement is a binary form, albeit asymmetrical (part two represents a more substantial development of the material from part one). Each part of the design can be partitioned into three sections. The texture of section one (mm. 1–13 for part one and 28–60 for part two) is quite contrapuntal, where the realization of a particular row by one instrument is imitated by another instrument playing a different row.

Section two (mm. 14–18 for part one and 68–74 for part two) uses rows II/C and II/D as the basis for a new imitative passage—however, in part one this imitation is supported by a presentation of movement one's row I/A by the cello and in part two, by row II/B, played by the viola.

Finally, section three (mm. 19–27 for part one and 75–80 for part two) is a homophonic passage in which harmonies derived from row I/A are played by the cello in double stops, while the first violin plays a realization of rows II/C and II/D.

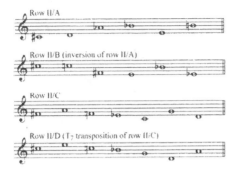

Figure 8.9 Row forms of String Quartet No. 1, mov. 2

Movement Three

The final movement, marked *Allegro non troppo*, is, like the first, a sonata-form design.   Further, with the exception of one passage in the recapitulation, the pitch material is derived from the three rows shown in Figure 8.10 (rows III/A and III/B are inversionally related to each other).

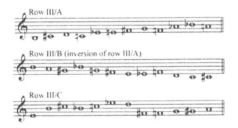

Figure 8.10 Row forms of String Quartet No. 1, mov. 3

The movement opens with a vigorous theme, shown in Figure 8.11. Of interest is the accompaniment generated from movement one's row I/A, played by the viola and cello. The loud dynamic and energetic opening dissipates to the second theme beginning at m. 26 and based upon row III/C. The theme is imitated between the two violins and the cello, using different rhythmic values; row III/A is used as supporting material.

Figure 8.11 String Quartet No. 1, mov. 3, mm. 1–5

The development begins at m. 67; it contains three sections, each of which features one of the three rows; at any one time the other two rows function as accompanimental support or as the basis for imitative textures. The recapitulation of themes one and two is not notably different from their appearance in the exposition. However, an important diversion from the exposition involves the interesting passage from mm. 196–224: following the presentation of the initial portion of theme two by the solo cello there is a recapitulation of important thematic ideas from the other two movements, using their respective associated rows. The remainder of theme two appears at m. 225 immediately following the interpolated section and segues to the culminating passage of the movement (mm. 248–254), one where an octave realization of row III/C by the first violin and cello is supported by the second violin and viola playing row III/A. The movement ends quietly with three A Major repeated triads—a surprising feature, given the paucity of tertian sonorities throughout the movement.

String Quartet No. 2

Kokkonen began work on his second quartet in late 1964. His original intention was that this quartet be a single-movement passacaglia. However, an illness during February of 1965 halted progress on the work for several months. When he returned to the piece during the summer months Kokkonen realized that his conception of the composition had expanded: while the original passacaglia idea was retained, it became positioned as the first of four movements. Ultimately, the quartet was completed in the spring of 1966; it was premiered by the Bastiaan Quartet on 10 October 1966.

The opening passacaglia is followed by a second-movement *Intermezzo*, a third movement *Allegro vivace* (preceded by an *Andante* introduction), and a fourth movement *Adagio*. Overall, there is a somber quality to the quartet: only the light-hearted *Intermezzo* stands in contrast to the severity of the other movements.   In fact, the complex textures, consistently dissonant harmonic language and long, angular melodies make Kokkonen's second quartet the most enigmatic and austere from his quartet cycle and among the most rigorous from his entire oeuvre—features which have no doubt contributed to its lesser familiarity when compared with the popularity of its two siblings.

Movement One

The passacaglia-designed first movement is largely based upon the row ordering row I/A shown in Figure 8.12 (the P_0 row form is illustrated). An interesting feature of the row's ordering is the tritone symmetry of the pitch classes from each hexachord: for example, C-C♯ and G-F♯, both interval-class 1s, are matched together; C♯-B and F-G, both interval-class 2s, are matched, etc.   The row's symmetry suggests an indebtedness to the celebrated row from the first movement of Berg's *Lyric Suite*, i.e., F,E,C,A,G,D,A♭,D♭,E♭,G♭,B♭,B, a composition Kokkonen is known to have admired a great deal. For instance, a reordering of each hexachord from Berg's row generates an incomplete interval-5 cycle (i.e., E-A-D-G-C-F from hexachord 1 and B♭-E♭-A♭-D♭-G♭-B from hexachord 2), a feature which Berg fully exploits in his work. By contrast, each hexachord from Kokkonen's row ordering contains an incomplete interval-1 cycle: B-C-C♯-D-D♯-E from hexachord 1 and F-F♯-G-G♯-A-B♭ from hexachord 2. Not only are these hexachordal relationships developed in the work, but they are noteworthy for they anticipate similarly designed row orderings found in a number of Kokkonen's later works—for instance, the Woodwind Quintet and Cello Sonata.

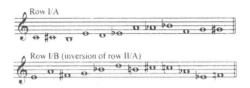

Figure 8.12 Row forms of String Quartet No. 2, mov. 1

The inherent symmetry of the row's structure may be interpreted as an analogue for the symmetry of the movement's overall formal design. Consider, for instance, the passacaglia statements themselves. As is well known, the traditional means to construct a series of passacaglia variations is to use a recurring melody as the basis from which melodic and harmonic elaboration is presented. A common strategy is to present the recurring melody in the baseline and, after a number of repetitions, it might migrate to the upper voices, thereby reducing the harmonic limitations inherent within the lower voice. The length of the passacaglia "theme" is typically identical, thereby providing a sense of consistency to the events of the variations (although deviations are certainly common—less so, however, during the beginning stages of a composition).

The design of the first movement diverges significantly from these conventions. First, while the passacaglia theme consists of a particular twelve-tone row ordering, the theme changes, as it is based upon several row forms, notably, P_0, I_0, P_4 and I_4. Second, while the passacaglia theme is used as a baseline, it is more often found as a *Klangfarben* melody between several instruments in an upper voice. Third, the length of these passacaglia variations changes constantly. The number of measures of each variation is based upon successive elements of a Fibinocci number series; the pattern to the number of measures is $3 - 5 - 8 - 13 - 8 - 5 - 3$ (there are occasional deviations to this model). The pattern of an increase and decrease of measure numbers occurs three times and forms the basis of the movement's arch-form design. Specifically, as the number of measures of each variation from the outer parts increases, there is a concomitant increase in rhythmic activity, overall dynamic and exploration of instrumental tessitura; these musical attributes diminish with a decrease in the number of measures of each variation. As a means of contrast, however, the middle part reverses this pattern: as the number of measures of each variation increases, there is a decrease in dynamic, rhythmic activity and instrumental range, only to increase as the section comes to a close. Table 8.1 outlines each variation from the three sections. Each row on the chart provides the following information for each passacaglia statement: the length (in measures); the measure numbers corresponding with each theme; the row forms and row orderings used; and the instrument(s) used to play the passacaglia theme.

The pattern of rows used for the various passacaglia statements also correlates with the just discussed tripartite arch form generated from such surface features as dynamics, tessitura, etc. For instance, the passacaglia themes are exclusively generated from the P_0 form of row I/A until the latter portion of part one. By contrast, the majority of the row forms used for the various passacaglia themes in part two utilize P_4 and I_4. Part three's immediate use of row form P_0 stimulates a sense of familiarity to the harmonic structure used during the outset of the movement (note, however,

Table 8.1 Formal design of String Quartet No. 2, mov. 1

Part One

Measure no.	Length (measures)	Row form	Instruments used for passacaglia theme
1–3	3	P_0	All instruments used, with a variety of colours.
4–8	5	P_0	Cello and violin 1 (violin 2 included at end of variation).
9–16	8	P_0	Exclusively by cello.
17–30	*14*	P_0	Exclusively by cello.
31–37	*7*	P_0	Viola and cello.
38–42	5	P_4	Violin 1.
	3		(Not contained in Section I.)

Part Two

Measure no.	Length (measures)	Row form	Instruments used for passacaglia theme
43–45	3	P_4	All instruments used simultaneously.
46–50	5	P_4	Cello and violin 1.
51–58	8	I_0	Viola and cello.
59–71	13	P_0	Viola and cello.
72–79	8	P_4	Shared between all instruments.
80–84	5	I_4	I_4 played by violin 1; P_4 (mov. 2) played by viola and cello.
85–89	*5*	I_0	Shared between all instruments.
90–92	3	P_4 and P_4/P_0	Shared between all instruments as chords, followed by statements of T_4 and T_0.

Part Three

Measure no.	Length (measures)	Row form	Instruments used for passacaglia theme
93–95	3	I_0	Violin 1 and cello.
96–100	5	I_4	Violin 1.
101–109	8	P_0	Cello.
110–121	13	P_0	Shared by all instruments.
122–129	8	P_0	Violin 1 and violin 2.
130–134	5	P_4	Shared by all instruments.

that part three also contains one instance of the related I_0, as well as one instance each of P_4, a row form also found in part one, and its related I_4).

Row I/B is a second row ordering of significance, not only for the movement, but, ultimately, the work as a whole. Often the row is used as harmonic support for the surface elaborations derived from row I/A's P_0, I_0, and to a lesser degree, P_4 and I_4. In part two, however, row I/B becomes progressively more prominent as the primary surface material; by m. 59, row I/B takes center stage. (In Figure 8.13, the passacaglia statement is shared between the viola and cello using row I/A; row II/B is played by the first and second violins).

An examination of the three row forms from row I/A, i.e., P_0, I_0, and P_4, illuminates important pitch-class interactions not only amongst themselves but also with the primary row form of row I/B, P_4. Such relationships with a row form that is so vital to the structure of the second movement, and overtly at the central point in the passacaglia, illustrate how specific row forms from carefully constructed row orderings can be a powerful strategy to achieve coherent intra-, as well as inter-movement harmonic associations.

Movement Two

Unlike the opening passacaglia, the pitch material of the second movement is entirely based upon the one row ordering in Figure 8.14; it is identical to movement one's row I/B. All four categories of row forms, i.e., Prime, Inversion, Retrograde Prime and Retrograde Inversion, are used; as we shall observe shortly, the deployment of specific row forms is an important means by which the movement's rondo design is articulated. For instance, consider mm. 1–5 from Figure 8.15: the first violin realizes P_4 in its characteristic contour and rhythm (the opening refrain (mm. 1–20) contains several instances of the particular realization of P_4, only placed in different registers); RP_5 immediately follows (RP_1 and I_9 are played by the second violin and the viola and cello, respectively, as support for the primary melodic material).

Figure 8.13 String Quartet No. 2, mov. 1, mm. 59–67

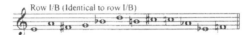

Figure 8.14 Row form of String Quartet No. 2, mov. 2

Figure 8.15 String Quartet No. 2, mov. 2, mm. 1–5

The first episode (mm. 21–44) is primarily based upon I and RI row forms; violin 1 plays the vast majority of the melodic material. While it should be noted that P_4 and RP_5 are realized during the central portion of the episode (mm. 31–36), the characteristic contour and rhythm of these rows forms heard in the opening refrain is absent, thus differentiating the material of these six measures from its earlier presentation.

The refrain reappears briefly in mm. 45–50, using the P_4 row form in the contour and register heard at the outset. A transition (mm. 51–54) to the second episode is based upon a realization of RI_0 played by the first violin.

Episode two (mm. 55–89) is itself an arch form design. The outer portions (mm. 55–58 and 85–89) contain a series of chords generated from P_4 and played by the viola and cello (mm. 55–58) in a characteristic rhythm—three triplet-eighth notes followed by a quarter note. The inner next portions (mm. 59–70 and 81–84) are distinguished by melodies constructed from I row forms played by the first violin in its higher registers. The central portion (mm. 71–80) is reminiscent of the first episode—namely, a passage built upon I and RI row forms that begins with sparse imitation between the four instruments and increases in dynamic level to *fortissimo*.

The final appearance of the refrain (mm. 90–107) contains one last realization of the P_4 row form (played by the viola) in its characteristic contour and rhythm. Surprisingly, given the absence of tertian sonorities in the movement, the rondo ends quietly with an A Major triad (however, the triad does contain an added pitch B).

Movement Three

The movement opens with a thirty-five measure introduction marked *andante* in tempo. The pitch material is derived from row III/A (all the rows from the movement appear in Figure 8.16). While the row ordering is new, the pitches from the opening tetrachord, {F♯,G,G♯,B}, have been heard in numerous guises from the two earlier movements. However, since many of the remaining row orderings in movements three and four emphasize the tetrachord, it proves to be an important link between the harmonic relationships from the first half of the work and the latter two movements.

Essentially, the introduction projects two arch-like melodies by the first violin; the apogee of the first melody is E6, while the second reaches C7. Corroborating with the enlarged register of the second melody is an increased dynamic level (*fortissimo* as opposed to the *forte* from the first melody) and a more contrapuntally complex texture supporting the towering violin line.

The *Allegro* movement proper begins at m. 36. Row III/B appears immediately at the outset, played by the first violin (shown in Figure 8.49); the contour and rhythm of the realization pervades the movement. Of significance is the opening tetrachord {B,F♯,G♯,G}: the four pitches are a reordering of the initial four pitches of row III/A, providing a harmonic association between the two rows. Two other rows are important for the movement's harmonic structure: (1) the P_4 row form of movement two's row ordering (row III/C); and (2) the inverted form of row III/B that begins on E (row III/D). The reordering of the opening tetrachord from row III/B becomes apparent when placed in context with the latter two rows. Specifically, the descending perfect 4th stands in contrast to the ascending perfect 4[ths] separating the first two pitches of rows III/C and III/D. However, the opening E-A ascending perfect 4th not only engenders a relationship between rows III/C and III/D (and as a corollary, between rows III/A and III/B) but additionally, harmonic associations with the portions of movements one and two that actively used rows I/B and II/A.

The movement is a ternary form. The pitch material of part A (mm. 36–110) is primarily based upon row III/B. At m. 59, however, row III/D becomes prominent and for the remainder of part A it either alternates with row III/B or is simultaneously stated with it. However, there is an interesting brief change in the interaction between rows III/B and III/D during mm. 76–81, when the registral spacing and slurring of the first six order positions of row III/C match exactly with its realization during the central segment of movement one, yet a further illustration of Kokkonen's attempt to garner inter-movement harmonic associations.

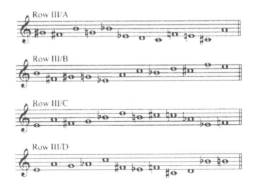

Figure 8.16 Row forms of String Quartet No. 2, mov. 3

Part B of the movement begins at m. 111 and is itself a ternary form. The outer sections (mm. 111–119 and 125–139) are homophonic in texture, where a variety of four-note harmonies are generated from row III/A. The middle section contains a brief alternation between rows III/B and III/C, reminiscent of the ending of part A.

A somewhat expansive transition to part A' begins at m. 140. Here, melodic realizations of rows III/A, III/B and III/D are supported with row

III/C played by the cello. Part A' begins at m. 167: although it is abridged in dimension when compared with part A, it recapitulates all the rhythms and contours that characterized the various row realizations earlier.

A coda begins at m. 201 and is consumed by row III/B: each of the instruments plays different segments of the row as the dynamic level gradually increases from *forte* to the triple *forte* that ends the movement.

Movement Four

All the pitch material for the *Epilogo* fourth movement, marked *Molto adagio*, is obtained from the two row orderings shown in Figure 8.17. Once again, the {B,F♯,G♯,G} tetrachord appears as the initial four order positions of row IV/A, preserving a valuable inter-harmonic relationship. A close study of rows IV/A and IV/B uncovers interesting harmonic relationships. For instance, row IV/B is "almost" a retrograde inversion of row IV/A (the order positions of D♭ and A♭ are switched). The slight change proves significant to differentiate the two rows: there are three semitones in the first hexachord (D♭-C, G♯-A and F♯-G)—a clear contrast with the perfect 4^{ths} in the first hexachord of row IV/A (B-F♯, G-C-F) or in the second half of row IV/B (F-B♭-E♭, E-B).

The movement is a ternary form. The pitch material from part A (mm. 1–7) is entirely generated from row IV/A and features imitation between the two violins that is supported from the double-stop chords by the viola and cello.

Figure 8.17 Row forms of String Quartet No. 2, mov. 4

In part B (mm. 10–16), the second violin realizes row IV/A in a triplet-sixteenth-note rhythm, while the other three instruments generate statements of row IV/B in slower rhythms.

Part A' begins in the latter half of m. 16 with imitation between the first violin and cello, using row IV/A in virtually the same contour as the opening (there is also imitation between the second violin and viola using row IV/B). The imitative passage leads to the movement's most dynamically forceful moment at m. 21, in which the two violins state row IV/A in a rhythmically augmented realization. The movement ends quietly with a sonority generated by the first six order positions from row III/A.

String Quartet No. 3

Kokkonen's third quartet dates from 1976, a particularly rich year that also saw the completion of the cello sonata as well as a significant amount of the work on *...durch einen Spiegel...* Along with their chronological proximity, the three works contain a similarity in dodecaphonic row structure—namely, pitch material that is primarily generated from hexachordal row orderings which are reordered partial chromatic scales (or more formally, an incomplete interval-1 cycle). In addition, the quartet contains numerous harmonic progressions that utilize tertian harmonies (but which are non-functional syntactically); these sonorities are particularly prevalent in the *Adagio* third movement.

The third quartet was premiered by the Finlandia Quartet on 24 August 1976. (As an interesting side note, the Finnish conductor and composer Leif Segerstam was the quartet's first violinist at the time.) The reception history of the quartet has been quite successful: not only is it the most performed quartet from Kokkonen's cycle of three, but it is also one of the most performed of all Finnish quartets.

Movement One

The *Allegretto* first movement is a three-rotation design followed by a short coda. Each rotation contains four sections. Section A features the first three rows shown in Figure 8.18a (Figure 8.18b illustrates the realization of the rows I/A, I/B and I/C in mm. 1–4). The harmonic trichord {A♭,G,C} is generated from the first three order positions of row I/A, and when combined with the characteristic rhythm illustrated, acts as a type of motto that marks the beginning of each new rotation.

In section B, a new row I/D and rhythmic motive appear; Figure 8.19 illustrates its typical realization—a simultaneous presentation with row I/B played by the two violins.

There are noteworthy alterations in section C. First, the rhythmic activity increases significantly with the numerous sixteenth figures (the figures are often played with a *marcato* articulation). The second change is that the rows are permuted to begin on different order positions with increasing frequency.

Section D is distinguished by two features. The first is the linking of rows I/A with I/F to form a thirteen-note row (a twelve-note row with one pitch repeated; the row is F♯,F,C,C♯,E,D,E♭,A♭,G,C,B,A,A♯). It functions as a passacaglia, upon which the other hexachordal rows are used as foreground material. A second feature is that retrograde versions of several rows begin to appear.

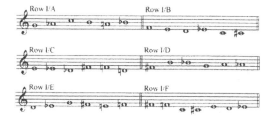

Figure 8.18a Row forms of String Quartet No. 3, mov. 1

Figure 8.18b String Quartet No. 3, mov. 1, mm. 1–4

Table 8.2 outlines the formal design of the movement. As is typical for movements in rotation-form design, general attributes established in the first rotation remain, but become manipulated to forge a sense of development in later rotations. For instance, the ordering of sections C and D is switched in rotation two, while in rotation three, component C is absent and components B and D appear at the same time. A further example involves the change in rhythmic interaction of rows I/B and I/D in section B between rotations one and two (a comparison between mm. 23–24 and m. 82 from rotation two is illuminating in this regard). Finally, consider the above-discussed thirteen-note row from section D. In rotation one the thirteen-note row is stated twice, doubled at the octave by the second violin and viola, and contains virtually no alterations to the registral positions of the pitches between the row statements. However, not only does rotation three contain six successive statements of the thirteen-note row, but the row's supportive role during the first few statements gradually changes to become the most vital feature in the latter two—largely due to the change in register from the cello's lowest octave to nearly three octaves above middle C by the violins in the sixth and final statement.

Table 8.2 Formal Design of String Quartet No. 3, mov. 1

Rotation:	I				II			III			
Measure no.:	1	17	30	51	63	75	83	112	133	137	170
Section:	A	B	C	D	A	B	D	C	A	B+D	Coda

Figure 8.19 String Quartet No. 3, mov. 1, mm. 23–24

Figure 8.20 Row forms of String Quartet No. 3, mov. 2

Movement Two

The pitch material from the second movement scherzo, marked *Allegro*, is derived from the row orderings shown in Figure 8.20. Row II/A accounts for the vast majority of the pitch material in the movement; row II/B, the inversional row form of row II/A, is of secondary importance. Both contain two chromatic hexachords: for instance, in row II/A, the first hexachord of the row contains a re-ordered chromatic scale from F-B♭, while the second hexachord contains the chromatic from B-E. Row II/C contains only eight pitches and is always realized as a series of harmonic dyads.

Figure 8.21 String Quartet No. 3, mov. 2, mm. 4–11

The movement is a ternary form. Part A is divided into two sections. In section one (mm. 1–19), a statement of row II/C is answered by an octave realization of row II/A by all four instruments; there are three such statement/response passages (Figure 8.21 illustrates the first). In section two (mm. 20–35), numerous statements of row II/A by the viola and cello (doubled in octaves) are supported by octatonic scalar material played by the two violins.

Although all three rows are used in part B, as contrast to the first part, row II/A is used minimally and row II/B features prominently (however, the row is consistently permuted so as to begin on the pitch B (i.e., B,D,D♭,E♭,C,E,F,A♭,F♯,G,A,B♭); a retrograde form of this permuted row also appears). As harmonic support, row II/C is presented by the second violin and viola as unmeasured tremolos.

The transition to part A' in mm. 47–55 combines both rows II/A and the permuted form of II/B used in part B. Part A' begins at m. 56. While the thematic ideas from the opening part are revisited, the increase in dynamic level, the greater registral expanse by the violins, and the numerous unmeasured tremolos generate a greater intensity to the ending when compared with part A. The movement ends with several repeated A Major triads played at a triple *forte* dynamic level.

Movement Three

The final movement, marked *Adagio*, contains a plethora of hexachordal row orderings; the rows are illustrated in Figure 8.22.

Figure 8.22 Row forms of String Quartet No. 3, mov. 3

The movement is a three-rotation design: rotation one is from mm. 1–22; rotation two, from mm. 23–43; and rotation three, from mm. 44–64 (Table 8.3 illustrates the formal design of the movement). Each rotation contains two sections: the first functions as a type of introduction to the second, more contrapuntally involved portion of the rotation. Rows III/A and III/B are featured in section one. Row III/B takes on a supporting role in the first and third rotations (by contrast, however, the row, realized by the cello, generates the primary melodic interest in the second rotation). The second section is somewhat more complex than the first, where different transpositions of rows III/A and III/C are in constant dialogue; further, rows III/A and III/D often appear simultaneously. The latter combination is interesting and recalls the grouping between the similarly designed rows I/A and I/D that appeared in each rotation of movement one.

Table 8.3 Formal Design of String Quartet No. 3, mov. 3

Rotation:	I		II		III	
Measure no.:	1	10	23	30	45	47
Section:	A	B	A	B	A	B

Two new features appear in rotation two. First, a new row III/E appears; it takes on an increasingly greater role throughout the remainder of the movement. Second, the ascending four-note motive played by the cello in mm. 17–18 that supported the above-discussed interaction between rows III/A and III/D now has a greater vibrant presence by the cello's series of perfect 5th double stops (it is valuable to compare two related passages from different rotations—for instance, mm. 40–42, as regards the changes in texture, dynamics and register).

The significance of the just-discussed perfect 5th double stops from the cello becomes extensively realized in the third rotation: although the ascending C♯-D-E-F motive is absent, the cello line articulates a triadic progression that supports an octave realization of row III/A by the violins. The movement ends calmly with a sustained E Major chord.

Woodwind Quintet

The origins of Kokkonen's Woodwind Quintet date from late 1971 on a commission from the Norwegian ensemble Den Norske Blåseqvintett. The work took nearly two years to complete, an unusual length of time and due largely to the diversions encountered from the work on *The Last Temptations* (the actual premiere of the quintet took place two years after the work was completed, on 15 April 1975, five months before the premiere of the opera). Kokkonen, however, has remarked that the lengthy genesis of the quintet was more than anything else the result of his changing compositional style. On first glance, it is perhaps difficult to capture the stylistic transformation to which Kokkonen refers: the pitch material of the quintet is nearly all generated from dodecaphonic procedures, where, like so many of Kokkonen's other serial works, different row orderings are used for divergent movements. Further, several of the rows have six pitches—again, not a unique feature, although there are a greater number in the quintet than in other prior works. However, what does make the quintet stand somewhat apart from Kokkonen's prior serial works is its much more integrated harmonic structure—and not just the associations between the rows within a movement, but also the vast number of inter-harmonic relationships. For instance, the majority of the pitch material from the first movement is generated from two transpositionally-related six-note rows. However, the two rows also exert a significant influence upon the design of the different row orderings from the other three movements. In addition, the two rows from movement one appear in these other movements as well, and their interaction with these row orderings plays a vital role in articulating the formal design of the work overall.

Movement One

As just identified, the majority of the pitch material from the movement is generated from the two six-note rows shown in Figure 8.23 (the retrograde forms are also used). Both rows are reordered chromatic hexachords that, when combined together, generate the entire chromatic aggregate.

Figure 8.23 Row forms of Woodwind Quintet, mov. 1

The movement is a ternary form: with the limited amount of pitch material in the two hexachordal rows, texture plays a significant role to provide formal contrast. For instance, part A contains two sections: each section opens with a *Klangfarben* realization of row I/A and is followed by a gradually increased polyphonic texture of imitative entries from realizations of both rows and their respective retrograde forms. Along with the increased polyphonic texture is a concomitant enlargement in instrumental doublings as well as simultaneous projections of different row forms. Figure 8.24 illustrates the opening measures of the movement.

Section two begins at m. 20. Like section one, it opens with a *Klangfarben* realization of row I/A (in mm. 20–25); however, it deviates from the earlier section by an even greater polyphonic texture. The density of imitative entries reaches its maximum in mm. 30–34, where all five instruments project simultaneously a particular row form.

Figure 8.24 Woodwind Quintet, mov. 1, mm. 1–12

Part B begins at m. 37 and is distinguished by: a more homophonic texture compared with the outer parts, more overt references to tertian sonorities, and the longer rhythmic values used to realize the different rows. For instance, the first phrase contains simultaneous realizations of different rows by the clarinet (row I/A), horn (row I/B) and bassoon (retrograde of row I/B); the opening chord is a G♭ Major triad, the enharmonic dominant of the final harmony of the phrase, B minor. Essentially, then, part B contains simultaneous statements by the clarinet, horn and bassoon that are immediately imitated by the flute and oboe. A return to the three lower voices is imitated by again the flute and oboe, only this time the rows originally played by the flute and oboe are exchanged.

The *Klangfarben* realization of row I/B at m. 50 demarcates the beginning of part A'. This part, however, contains only one section: following the initial *Klangfarben* presentation is the most extensive polyphonic passage in the movement, one where all five instruments realize simultaneously a row or its retrograde. A short coda begins at m. 60 and is based upon the imitative and rhythmic features of part B.

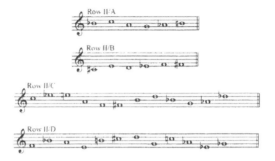

Figure 8.25 Row forms of Woodwind Quintet, mov. 2

Movement Two

The second movement is a ternary form; the pitch material from the outer parts is based upon the same two six-note rows from movement one (all the rows used in the movement are shown in Figure 8.25).

Three motives from the opening few measures prove significant for the entire movement: (1) a series of (usually four) repeating eighth notes played with a staccato articulation, in which each of the eighth notes is separated by an eighth-note rest; (2) a five-note figure that combines eighth and sixteenth notes; and (3) a figure of four sixteenth notes followed by an eighth note.

Part A is distinguished by extensive imitation of the two rows (and their respective retrograde forms) among the five instruments. However, the opening part is also characterized by an arch design, as regards to: (1) the density of information, i.e., the number imitative events per unit of time; (2) the overall rhythmic activity; and (3) the increased use of a higher register.

Part B begins at m. 35 and contains four phrases; each phrase contains a harmonic realization of row II/D cast in long rhythmic values; interval-class 5 features prominently among the harmonic dyads.

A transition to part A' begins at m. 72; the harmonic form of row II/D is now realized among several instruments and cast in a quarter-note rhythm. At m. 91 the motives used in part A reappear, as do rows II/A and II/B, demarcating the beginning of part A'. As a way of contrast with the opening part, however, row D reappears at m. 102 realized in a modified version of motive II. The addition of the latter row generates the multi-layered ending in which rows II/A, II/B, and II/D are simultaneously presented by all five instruments. A short coda (beginning at m. 142) presents an aggressive octave/unison realization of row II/C at a triple *forte* dynamic level by all the instruments except for the horn, which plays a realization of row II/A.

Movement Three

The design of the third movement is based upon two contrasting ideas. One scheme is the extensive interaction of the first two rows shown in Figure 8.26. Of note is the similarity between the realization of these rows and the Dance Hall music in act I – scene 2 from *The Last Temptations*). There is rarely an instance when at least two voices are not involved in presenting the two row forms; as such, an important means by which aural fatigue is avoided is by the continual changes in orchestration and register. A third row form (row III/C) is a retrograde of row III/A permuted to begin on the pitch D; despite the similarity of pitch content, rhythmic profile and articulation with row III/A, contrast is achieved by row III/C's inverted contour.

The second, contrasting idea vital to the movement's design is a homophonic chorale–styled passage, typically five measures in length. Although no row form is used, all twelve pitches are present.

Figure 8.26 Row forms of Woodwind Quintet, mov. 3

The formal design of the movement is seen in Table 8.4. Each of the A sections varies the realization of the materials identified above. The uniformity, as regards pitch, rhythm and orchestration, in association with its longer rhythmic values, engenders a cadence-like quality to B sections, when compared with the rather capricious quality of the melodic material from the A sections.

Table 8.4 Formal Design of Woodwind Quintet, mov. 3

Measure no.:	1–17	18–23	24–48	49–54	55–77	78–80	81–91	92–97
Section:	A	B	A	B	A	B	A	B

Movement Four

Although the fourth movement contains no distinct formal demarcations, it is possible to identify a four-part design, as regards texture (section one is from mm. 1–39; section two, mm. 40–56; section three, mm. 57–87; and section four, mm. 88–125). Specifically, each section begins with a sparse texture with imitation between rows I/A and I/B (from movement one) and progressively augments the number of imitative events as well as increases the number of different rows that are used. For instance, in section one, movement two's row II/D is added at m. 13 following the imitation between rows I/A and I/B. Row IV/A appears at m. 18: not only is the row consistently realized as a series of harmonic dyads between two instruments, but with each successive section, it becomes perceptibly more prominent throughout the movement (the row is shown in Figure 8.27). Section one ends with a passage (mm. 34–40), where three rows (i.e., I/A, II/D and IV/A) are simultaneously realized among the five instruments.

Figure 8.27 Row forms of Woodwind Quintet, mov. 4

Like the prior three sections, section four begins with imitation between rows I/A and I/B. Associated with the increase in orchestral activity, however, is a new feature in the movement, row IV/B: the row first appears at m. 96 and is used in virtually every measure until the end of the movement—in fact, between mm. 109 and 117 all five instruments are simultaneously used to realize the row. The movement ends with an aggressive triple *forte* octave/unison statement of row IV/B by all five instruments.

Cello Sonata

The three-movement Cello Sonata was written between 1975 and 1976, and along with the third string quartet, represents one of Kokkonen's final chamber works of import. It was written for the celebrated Finnish cellist Arto Noras, the musician for whom Kokkonen composed his Cello Concerto. Noras and the pianist Hadassa Schwimmer premiered the work in Basel on 3 April 1976.

Movement One

The first movement is a sonata form with an *andante* introduction. The five tone rows shown in Figure 8.28 generate a significant percentage of the pitch material in the movement (for instance, the introduction is primarily generated from rows I/A and I/B). The rows are closely related to one another: row I/B begins with a T_4 transposition of row I/A, then reverses the ordered pitch-class interval series of row I/A that begins on order position 10. The upshot is that the two rows sound as if they are transposed retrograde inversions of each other. Interestingly, these rows are primarily realized as harmonic sonorities apart from the introduction. However, melodic forms of these rows appear at significant moments in the other two movements, generating attractive inter-movement harmonic relationships.

Figure 8.28 Row forms of Cello Sonata, mov. 1

The introduction is a ternary form as regards the use of the two rows. Specifically, row I/A generates a significant percentage of the melodic material in the outer parts (mm. 1–19 and 41–50), while row I/B is featured in the middle part. Figure 8.29 reproduces the opening measures and illustrates three motivic ideas that appear not only in the introduction, but also throughout the movement: (1) a melodic realization of row I/A, here played by the cello; (2) a polyphonic melody, where one voice realizes row I/A (here played by the piano right hand); and (3) the tertian sonorities as harmonic support.

Figure 8.29 Cello Sonata, mov. 1, mm. 1–9

At m. 51, the tempo changes from *andante* to *allegro*, demarcating the exposition proper. Rows I/C and I/D dominate the first thematic area, although a further resource is the numerous fragments of row I/E (using both prime and retrograde forms of this row are used). The latter row, an inverted form of row I/C, is the primary resource for the second thematic area (beginning at m. 86 in the exposition and m. 165 in the recapitulation).

The development (mm. 115–146) also doubles as a cello cadenza (although the piano is occasionally used to identify cadential passages within the cadenza). Although comparably brief in duration, virtually every major motive from the exposition appears.

Measure 149 marks the beginning of the recapitulation: following a brief six-measure appearance of theme one, theme two is extensively developed. The cello plays the majority of the thematic material for both themes, using tertian sonorities from the piano as harmonic support.

A coda begins at m. 186. Rows I/A and I/B return, as do the motives that characterized the introduction—however, unlike the opening section, these motivic ideas are now cast at an *allegro* tempo.

Movement Two

The second movement, marked *Adagio*, is a tripartite formal design. The row orderings shown in Figure 8.30 generate much of the pitch material in the movement: row II/A is virtually identical to row I/A; row II/B is the inverted form of row II/A; while row II/C is a virtually identical retrograde form of row II/B. Row II/D presents a somewhat distinctive ordering from the other three rows; row II/E is nearly identical to row II/D. The upshot is that the movement contains two categories of harmonic relationship, as regards row orderings: the relationships between rows II/A, II/B and II/C (and the concomitant inter-harmonic associations with movement one) and the associations between rows II/D and II/E.

Figure 8.30 Row forms of Cello Sonata, mov. 2

Part A contains a succession of realizations of rows II/A, II/B and II/C, finally returning to II/A; each realization is harmonized by tertian triads (as an illustration, mm. 1–8 are shown in Figure 8.31). Each row statement is bridged by a fragment of row II/D.

Part B begins at m. 12 and features interaction between realizations of rows II/D (by the cello) and II/E (by the piano). There is a gradual increase in rhythmic activity and dynamic intensity by both instruments, leading to the culminating passage of the movement—a tertian harmonized version of row I/A, played at a triple *forte* dynamic level.

Part C begins at m. 37 with the same harmonization and dynamic level associated with row II/A's realization at the opening of the movement; fragments of row II/D, now stated in double stops by the cello, are used to mitigate the numerous realizations of row I/A. However, a particularly impressive passage combines various transpositions of a portion of row II/E, played by the cello (i.e., a harmonic element that characterized part B), with realizations of row II/C by the piano (a feature from part A). The movement ends quietly (the dynamic level is triple *piano*) with a final statement of row II/A played by the cello and harmonized by the piano with a realization that strongly recalls the opening measures.

Movement Three

The pitch material of the ternary-form final movement, marked *Allegretto mosso*, is primarily generated from the five row orderings illustrated in Figure 8.32. There are two categories of pitch relationship: specifically, rows III/A, III/B, and III/E, as well as rows III/C and III/D, share several order position associations, harmonic features that Kokkonen develops throughout the movement.

Figure 8.31 Cello Sonata, mov. 2, mm. 1–7

Figure 8.32 Row forms of Cello Sonata, mov. 3

The outer parts of the ternary design (the parts begin at m. 1 and m. 76) are characterized by interplay of a somewhat whimsical theme; the rhythm and contour of the theme pervade both outer parts. More specifically, however, the pitch material of these parts is primarily generated from various associations between rows III/A, III/B, III/C and III/D.

By contrast, the middle part, mm. 35–75, features row III/E in long rhythmic values; the realization of this row is harmonically supported by various transpositions of a hexachord obtained from row III/A.

Improvvisazione

Improvvisazione is a short work for violin and piano written on commission for an international violin competition held in the United States at Indiana University in 1982. *Improvvisazione* was not only Kokkonen's final chamber work, but also one of his last compositions altogether: the only completed works that followed include a short choral work from 1985 and the 1987 chamber orchestra piece *Il paesaggio*.

Figure 8.33 Row forms of *Improvvisazione*

Improvvisazione contains an interesting bipartite design. Part one, mm. 1–60, is a ternary design that is largely based upon row A (the two primary row orderings of the work are illustrated in Figure 8.33); although several row forms are utilized (for instance, the inversional form beginning on E♭, i.e., I₃, is frequently used), the row form illustrated (i.e., P₁₁) is the most common. Section a consists of a succession of realizations of row A: each statement is not only rhythmically different, but also placed higher in register—the piece opens with the violin placed in its lowest register; by m. 25 it reaches its highest octave. Associated with these changes in register, however, is a gradual rhythmic diminution of the material by both instruments, engendering a subtle rhythmic acceleration to the section overall.

Section b, mm. 35–40, features the violin alone (although the piano plays occasional chords as punctuation to the violin's material) with *marcato*-styled double stops intercut with rapid scalar figures; transpositions of row A are used. Section a' (mm. 41–57) repeats the design of the opening—however, the violin's registral ascent is more rapid and does not contain the earlier process of rhythmic diminution.

Following a brief transition for violin alone, part two begins at m. 61. An increase in tempo (from ♩ = 72–80 to ♩. = 100) corresponds with the meter change from ⁴₄ to ⁶₈. Row B is now the primary resource from which the pitch material for the remainder of the piece is obtained. Part two is also a ternary form; as a means of differentiation, however, the pattern to the design is reversed from part one. Specifically, the outer sections (mm. 61–114 and 133–154) are characterized by numerous syncopated rhythmic figures and rapid sixteenth-note scalar patterns, played by both instruments over the top of the piano's left-hand ostinato. The middle section, marked *Un poco tranquillo*, contrasts with the outer sections, not only with its slower tempo (♩. = 80), but also its much longer rhythmic setting of the violin's melody.

Chapter 9

Keyboard Works

As recounted in chapter two, Kokkonen was essentially self-taught as a composer: the only extensive formal musical training he received at the Sibelius Academy, aside from classes in theory and history, was on the piano, where he studied with the Finnish pianist Ilmari Hannikainen. Indeed, Kokkonen began his musical career not as a composer but, rather, as a concert pianist and during the 1940s and 1950s developed a level of recognition in Finland, particularly as a performer of Beethoven, Brahms, Chopin, and Mozart. Kokkonen's performances also included Bach, and it was from his first-hand experience with his keyboard works that Kokkonen developed his life-long admiration and passion for the Baroque master's compositions.

Given his predilection towards the piano, probably the most surprising feature of Kokkonen's oeuvre is the lack of emphasis the instrument plays in his post-1957 works: while the piano featured centrally in all of his early compositions—there is not a single pre-*Music for String Orchestra* work that does not utilize the piano—once he found his compositional voice and recognized that his talents rested with large-scale composition, for the most part he abandoned the piano. In total, there are less than ten works that even have a piano part at all (this number includes orchestral works such as *Opus Sonorum* and the third symphony), and only one work at all for solo piano.

This chapter examines a handful of Kokkonen's keyboard works: aside from two relatively minor organ compositions, three piano works are discussed: the second composition he ever penned, the 1938 *Pielavesi*; the 1953 Sonatina, a work appearing at the threshold of Kokkonen's stylistic change to dodecaphonic composition; and his Five Bagatelles from 1968, a work written after his third symphony, another watershed work in his oeuvre.

Pielavesi

Dating from 1939, the title of this five-movement suite stems from the small island by the same name where Kokkonen's Brother Veijo and sister-in-law Ester had a summer cottage; the work bears their names in the dedication. Kokkonen used to spend some of his summer vacation at this cottage during the 1930s; as such, the five movements are programmatic musical portraits of his experiences from this idyllic setting.

Although the manuscript was never destroyed, the work remained unperformed for decades and was only published after Kokkonen's death. His suppression of the work, however, should not be surprising. Even though the notoriously self-critical composer felt *Pielavesi* was an important enough work to prevent it from suffering the fate of his fireplace, it is not difficult to surmise that Kokkonen would have found such a richly programmatic work from his youth antithetical (and perhaps even somewhat embarrassing) to the modernist views he espoused throughout the majority of his career.

Preludietto

The first movement, marked *Molto moderato*, is a ternary form. An ostinato generated from a sixteenth-note sextuplet figure forms the harmonic basis for the left-hand melody doubled in thirds. The opening measures from part A are illustrated in Figure 9.1: of note is the dominant to tonic bass note motion articulating an E♭ tonality; as noted elsewhere, this particular bass motion is an unusual feature in Kokkonen's music. Part B begins at m. 26 and retains a piano texture similar to the outer parts—i.e., a right-hand ostinato and a left-hand melody played as a combination of octaves and thirds; however, the tonality has shifted a semitone to E Major (although, interestingly, there is a prominent focus upon the pitch G♯ that pervades this middle part). A somewhat unremarkable recapitulation of part A begins at m. 43 and calmly brings the movement to an end on an E♭ Major triad.

Nocturne

The second movement, marked *Un poco sostenuto e dolcissimo*, is a rondo design. The refrain is a curious mix of a B Major ostinato figure in the left hand and a right-hand melody doubled in fifths suggesting the relative minor key of G♯ minor.

The first episode begins at m. 10: its chorale-like texture contains a tonal focus upon E♭ Major (although the tonic is only stated occasionally; more often, E♭ is implied by the dominant harmony that ends a phrase). A second episode beginning at m. 25 contains a lilting dance-like passage in B♭ Major.

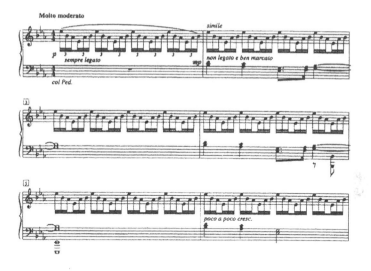

Figure 9.1 *Pielavesi*, **Preludietto, mm. 1–6**

The two episodes appear in succession again—the first episode from mm. 31–37 and mm. 42–54, the second episode from mm. 38–41—before the return of the refrain at m. 55. A coda begins at m. 62 and features the chorale-like material of the first episode with a tonal focus of E♭ Major. Curiously, the movement ends on C Major.

Sade (Rain)

The third movement, marked *Veloce e espressivo*, is a ternary form; the outer parts articulate a tonal focus of F♯ minor. The tempo and relentless sixteenth-note figure that characterize the piece (and programmatically, a relentless summer rain shower) engender a toccata-like feel to the work.

Triplet-sixteenth arpeggio figures in mm. 48–58 and mm. 77–91 frame part B, one that articulates an F minor tonality. The middle part is further distinguished by containing the only real melodic gesture in the movement. The figures articulating F♯ minor near the end of the movement gradually decrease in tempo and lead to the final sustained F♯ Major triad—a metaphor for the ray of sunshine that has now appeared.

Iltapilviä (Clouds at Evening)

Movement four, marked *Andantino semplice*, is another rondo design. The refrain consists of a repeating B♭ minor triad cast in a constant syncopated quarter-note rhythm; the left hand, however, states the melodic material. The first episode begins at m. 23: a new four-note ostinato played by the left hand implies B♭; the right hand plays a series of harmonies that alternate between the dominant 7th of E♭ and the dominant 7th of A♭.

The refrain returns at m. 40: aside from occasional changes in register of the repeating B♭ minor triad, the most significant alteration is the additional harmonization of the left-hand melody. A second episode begins at m. 59: although the section does not contain a B Major triad, the numerous instances of the key's dominant 7th harmony ({F♯,A♯,C♯,E}) and five-sharp key signature suggests a tonal center of B Major. Like the first episode, an ostinato is placed in the left hand and the melody in the right. However, melodic lines from both parts are doubled in thirds.

Both episodes return almost verbatim at m. 77 (episode one) and m. 96 (episode two). The refrain appears one final instance at m. 107; the left-hand melody is not harmonized and virtually identical to its initial appearance.

Aamutuuli (Morning Wind)

The final movement, marked *Vivacissimo*, is a ternary form. Part A begins at m. 7 following the opening flurry of sixteenth-note arpeggios; it contains three motives that feature prominently in the piece: a trill figure, a rising six-note chromatic scalar figure, and a series of triads (the latter motive immediately follows the chromatic figure). Part B begins at m. 42 and contains two sections: section one is an elaborated descending scalar passage; section two begins at m. 50 and contains a right-hand ostinato of harmonic dyads in quarter-note rhythm and an elaborated scalar passage cast in a triplet eighth-note rhythm.

Following a repetition of part B (section one begins at m. 71, section two at m. 79) is an exact repetition of Part A. A coda begins at m. 127: it consists of a chorale cast in a half-note rhythm that brings the movement calmly to an end on a B♭ Major triad.

Sonatina

The three-movement Sonatina was composed in 1953 and premiered on 26 October 1953 in Helsinki by Kokkonen himself at the first concert completely devoted to his music. The manuscript was subsequently lost after a recording Kokkonen then made for the Finnish Radio Company shortly after the concert. After several broadcasts of the work, Kokkonen had to somehow fulfill the numerous requests he received for a copy of the music and thus re-wrote the piece from memory; the only substantive change was the addition of the *adagio* introduction to the third movement.

Movement One

The first movement, marked *Adagio*, is a ternary form (part B begins at m. 11; part A' at m. 17). The outer parts are based upon a five-harmony chaconne played by the left hand; the right hand plays a three-phrase melody (there are three statements of the melody in the opening part; two in the final part). Figure 9.2 illustrates the chaconne series and the first statement of the three-phrase melody in mm. 1–5.

Figure 9.2 Sonatina, mov. 1, mm. 1–5

Part B contrasts with the outer parts in several ways. First, a *forte* dynamic dominates, as opposed to the *pianissimo* dynamic from the outer parts. Second, the left hand plays only one harmony—D Major. Third, the right-hand melody is essentially a single phrase with three varied repetitions.

Movement Two

Movement two, marked *Allegro*, is also in a ternary form, albeit more complex than the first movement. The outer parts of the form consist of several varied statements of the theme shown in Figure 9.3. There are two important motives: the ascending portion of the theme (the emphasis upon perfect 4^{ths} is noteworthy) and the descending portion derived from the octatonic collection OCT$_{2,3}$; both motives are extensively developed throughout the movement. By contrast, part B (mm. 25–76) is a series of elaborated repetitions of another interval-class 5 rich theme.

Figure 9.3 Sonatina, mov. 2, mm. 1–3

Movement Three

The final movement contains a six-measure *adagio* introduction; the passage recapitulates the same five-chord chaconne and melodic material from movement one. The movement proper is a binary design in which part B is an elaborated version of part A. Each part, however, is subdivided into two sections; each section is differentiated by a distinctive interval-class 5 rich theme.

Five Bagatelles

Written between 1968 and 1969, the Five Bagatelles represent Kokkonen's most important keyboard work overall and the most ambitious contribution for the instrument following the 1957 *Music for String Orchestra*. The work was premiered on 21 April 1969 by the Swedish pianist Gunnar Sjöström at the Levande Musik Nordic festival.

Praeambulum

The two tone rows shown in Figure 9.4 generate the majority of the pitch material in the first movement: row A contains eleven pitches; row B, ten. While the registral positions of these rows frequently change, their contour remains virtually intact throughout the piece. However, despite the consistent shape of the two rows, there are significant differences. First, row A is realized both melodically and harmonically, row B only melodically. Second, row B is virtually always realized in its entirety (the final pitch is occasionally eliminated). Row A, however, is often divided into two segments which are manipulated somewhat freely: the entire row may be stated in retrograde or the second segment may appear first. Despite the changes, however, the contour of the two portions remains preserved. Figure 9.5 illustrates the interaction between the two rows in mm. 1–7.

There are three particular realizations of row A that are supported by an arch-designed contour of chromatic motion played by the left hand; the scalar motion is harmonized by perfect 5^{ths} (Figure 9.5 contains the first realization from mm. 8–11). In each instance, the row statement by the right hand appears at the same pitch level. The recurring passage engenders a sense of stability to the movement amidst the numerous other realizations of rows A and B which are cast in a variety of registers and rhythms, contributing to the improvisatory quality of the movement.

Figure 9.4 Row forms of Five Bagatelles, Praeambulum

Figure 9.5 Five Bagatelles, Praeambulum, mm. 1–14

Andantino

The pitch material of the ternary-form second movement is based upon the nine-element row shown in Figure 9.6. Except for two, two-measure cadential gestures in which both hands play the same melodic material at a distance of two octaves, the row is completely confined to the right hand and realized in a variety of different rhythms and registers.

By way of contrast, however, the left hand consistently maintains a four-note ostinato in which the tetrachord {C♯,G♯,A,B♭} has a prominent role ({A♭,E♭,E,F}, a T₇ related tetrachord, appears occasionally); significantly, the tetrachord contains the three missing pitches from the nine-note row.

Figure 9.6 Row form of Five Bagatelles, Andantino

Measures 20–31 contrast significantly with the remainder of the movement: the row is realized as harmonic dyads played by both hands; T₅ and T₇ transpositional relationships appear frequently.

Aves

Aves is one of the few programmatic pieces that Kokkonen acknowledged. As he recounted in the original program notes of the work:

> This is one of my few distinctly programmatic works. Ever since I was a boy, birds and trees have in some way symbolized eternity for me. It was a very sunny, frosty morning, and outside our living room window a flock of birds, yellow hammers, was fluttering restlessly. There were some grains of corn in the snowdrift, and the flock of birds kept swirling down to feed and returning to the branch of a nearby tree. I followed the birds' games. Suddenly one of them flew into the glass of the window and was killed. This shocked me: the destruction of the life of the tiny bird. This is what provided the subject for the movement called *Aves*, and the haphazard nature of the birds' flight, its spontaneous and sudden nature.

The basic building block of the movement is a symmetrical tetrachord, and specifically, the tetrachord whose interval pattern (in semitones) is 1-2-1—in other words, the same both forwards and backwards (for instance, the tetrachord {C,C♯,D♯,E}). Three such tetrachords dominate the movement:

{C,C♯,D♯,E}, {F,F♯,G♯,A} and {G,G♯,A♯,B}. These tetrachords are utilized both in isolation as well as concatenated into a series to generate scalar passages.

There are two further important pitch-class sets in Aves— {C,C♯,D,D♯,E} and {G,G♯,A,A♯,B}. While they are obviously related to the {C,C♯,D♯,E} and {G,G♯,A♯,B} tetrachords, there are two distinguishing features of the pentachords: (1) a characteristic contour of <-1,+2,-3,-1>[1]; and (2) much longer rhythmic values.

The symmetrical structure of the tetrachords and pentachords may be interpreted as an analogue of Aves' symmetrical formal design. The movement opens with various realizations of the three tetrachords that alternate with scalar passages generated from the concatenation of the three tetrachords. A contrasting part B, mm. 31–68, is based upon the just described tetrachord/pentachord interaction. There is a brief cessation of this rhythmically active interaction in mm. 49–55 with a series of harmonic progressions based upon eight-note harmonies. At m. 69, the alteration between scalar passages and the three tetrachords that characterized part A returns; the section culminates at m. 92 with an eight-note chord, played triple *forte*, a musical metaphor for the fate of the unfortunate bird. The movement ends quietly with a repetition of a harmonic progression from the middle portion of part B.

Elegiaco

The pitch material of the *Adagio* fourth movement is based upon the three rows shown in Figure 9.7 (the retrograde forms of all three rows are also used): rows A and B are always presented melodically, row C harmonically. Row A is the most prevalent—in fact, aside from the first portion of m. 17 (both left and right hands play row B), there is no moment when row A cannot not heard. By contrast, row C is heard minimally: aside from the right-hand presentations in m. 4 and the last two measures, the only other instances of row C are played by the left hand in mm. 10–12 and 19–20. However, the dynamic levels of the two latter passages are *forte* and *fortissimo*, respectively, suggesting an association between the harmonies from row C and the most dynamically aggressive moments in the score.

Arbores

Arbores is a departure from the earlier four movements, as regards dodecaphonic technique. Specifically, row A, shown in Figure 9.8, is cast as a passacaglia, with repetitions confined to the piano's lowest register and consistently realized in the contour illustrated. The movement is a two-part design. In part one, mm. 1–33, the passacaglia theme supports alternating statements of the two other rows: row B is always presented as a series of harmonic dyads; row C is melodic in character. However, like the passacaglia theme, the register and specific contour of the two rows are fixed (although there are occasional, slight alterations to individual pitches).

Figure 9.7 Row forms of Five Bagatelles, Elegiaco

Figure 9.8 Row forms of Five Bagatelles, Arbores

In part two, mm. 34–57, the tempo changes from *Molto adagio* to *Poco largamente*. While the same three rows are used, they are now realized in a manner that generates simultaneous, different layers of information. Specifically, one layer results from duplicating the "passacaglia" row A at a space of four octaves; the extreme distance between the lines establishes the registral boundaries of aural information. A second layer utilizes the four octaves of the piano outlined in layer one and employs the following: (1) row B, again as a series of harmonic dyads; (2) row C by both hands in octave duplication; and (3) fragments of row A, again duplicated at the octave. Figure 9.9 illustrates the realization of these layers in mm. 34–40.

Figure 9.9 Five Bagatelles, Arbores, mm. 34–40

Surusoitto

Surusoitto (*Sorrowful Music*) is a short organ work written in 1969 as a tribute to Kokkonen's mother who died the same year; the work was performed by Kokkonen himself at the funeral service on 14 June 1969. Like *Hääsoitto* from a year earlier, *Surusoitto* is a ternary form design, in which the outer parts are a rounded binary form. The tonal focus is E Major (there is an exact da capo repetition of the opening section) and the contrasting middle part is a series of short phrases with a tonal focus of B minor.

    Surusoitto's significance extends beyond its utilitarian function, however: the work's recurring melody and chord progression served as the primary material for the *Adagio* third movement of the Cello Concerto.

Luxta crucem

This seven-minute organ work dates from 1979 and can best be described an oddity, given its position within Kokkonen's oeuvre. Specifically, the composition is much more dissonant than any other of the composer's works from the 1970s and 1980s, due largely to the paucity of tertian-styled triads.

Virtually all the pitch material in *Luxta crucem* is generated from the two row orderings shown in Figure 9.10. Although a number of transpositions of both rows and their respective inversional forms are used, the most prevalent are the two shown.

Figure 9.10 Row forms of *Luxta crucem*

The work is a type of fantasia, where a plethora of realizations of the two row orderings alternate in succession. The various realizations lead to two analogous chorale-like passages in mm. 44–56 and mm. 70–80: in both instances row A is placed in the soprano voice and harmonized by tertian-styled triads. The longer rhythmic values in the passage, as well as the cessation of rhythmic activity that anticipates them, suggests that these chordal passages function as formal markers, establishing an underlying two-part design to the fantasia.

One final note of interest. Both row orderings are used in approximately equal fashion by the manuals. However, except for one brief instance, only row A is ever utilized by the foot pedals, suggesting that Kokkonen perhaps placed slightly greater importance upon this particular row ordering.

Luxta crucem was premiered by Aimo Känkänen on 8 August 1979 in Lahti, Finland.

Note

1. The integers refer to semitones; by convention, the angle brackets surrounding the series of integers designate a specific ordering. An example of this particular contour would be: <C,B,C,B♭,A>.

Chapter 10

Kokkonen's Legacy

Kokkonen belongs to the generation of composers born just after World War I and who came to prominence during the 1950s; the cohort includes such celebrated names as Pierre Boulez, Luciano Berio, György Ligeti and Karlheinz Stockhausen (to name but four). For these composers and their followers, innovation was a fundamental premise of their music. Although Kokkonen was certainly aware of these composers as well as the major European music trends during the 1940s and 1950s—as early as 1949 the Society for Contemporary Music in Helsinki began performing this music and inviting composers from continental Europe to give lectures—he was never the relentless experimentalist that such modernists have shown to be throughout their respective careers (although as I have identified in numerous analyses throughout this book, Kokkonen's particular approach to dodecaphonic composition is an unusual and fascinating contribution that needs to be more extensively studied). Kokkonen further cast himself apart from mainstream European musical activities through a determined avoidance of electronic music composition throughout his career. Instead, he embraced his country's tradition of orchestral music that begins essentially with Sibelius and has played such a vital role in twentieth-century Finnish culture and never strayed from an aesthetic of narrative structure and expression that has been a part of western art music for centuries—one which was shunned for a time by post-World War II composers—where expression and significance in a composition arise from the presentation of a linked series of events.

Kokkonen's 1957 *Music for String Orchestra* is a watershed work in his oeuvre. First, the composition garnered him recognition within the Finnish musical community as an important orchestral composer—a striking point to consider, since the piece is widely considered one of the finest examples of post-World War II string ensemble writing and yet, remarkably, was the first orchestral work he penned. However, *Music for String Orchestra* also represents an important evolutionary stage away from the neoclassically styled piano, voice and piano, or chamber works from the prior two decades. Specifically, *Music for String Orchestra* is Kokkonen's first foray into dodecaphonic composition; as we saw in the discussion of the piece, two of the four movements are dodecaphonically constructed. However, what is particularly impressive is that an interesting characteristic that features prominently in the vast majority of the post-1957 works, i.e., to utilize multiple, different row orderings within a movement, is not an attribute with which he struggled to develop over a period of time; it was formulated even within his initial twelve-tone composition.

With an astonishing series of orchestral compositions written between 1957 and 1962, i.e., *Music for String Orchestra*, *The Hades of the Birds*, the first two symphonies, and *Sinfonia da camera*, Kokkonen was swiftly catapulted to the forefront of musical activities in Finland; the rise in fame led to his appointment to the Finnish Academy of Sciences in 1963 (the position had been made vacant with Uuno Klami's untimely death in 1961). While the value and importance of these works has never been in question, it should be noted that they appeared at a particularly critical time in Finland's history. Specifically, Sibelius' death in 1957 had left a cultural vacuum in place which Kokkonen's works, and, notably, his two symphonies, played a vital role in filling. For instance, not only did these works utilize a mode of pitch construction which was then in vogue (as was recounted in chapter one, many works from the 1950s by composers such as Eric Bergman and Einojuhani Rautavaara utilized extensive twelve-tone procedures), but these pitch materials were incorporated within a compositional aesthetic strongly influenced by Sibelius.

For nearly three decades, Kokkonen was viewed as Finland's pre-eminent living composer, whose cycle of symphonies continues to be considered the most vital set of essays after Sibelius; as such, he holds an important position in the lineage of twentieth-century Finnish orchestral music. Specifically, Kokkonen entered the world of symphonic composition (and, as was noted earlier, at a relatively late age) at a time when it was all but considered passé by the musical avant-garde from that time. His success played an important part in reestablishing a prominent role for symphonic composition in the Finnish concert hall after nearly a decade of diminished interest in the genre. Further, as has been remarked earlier, his opera *The Last Temptations* is the most successful Finnish opera of all time. However, his compositions are only one part of the picture that explicates Kokkonen's stature: his political role in Finnish culture was also central, as he either chaired or maintained a prominent role in a number of significant boards, both within Finland, as well as internationally. His position on these various boards played an extremely important part in improving grant systems and fair copyright structures for composers, as well as the development of an early music education system that is arguably the most advanced in Europe today. Because of his pervasive presence, both within the concert hall as well as many political forums, for a time Kokkonen achieved that all too rarified position for a classical composer—that of a household name. However, as might be expected, Kokkonen's extensive—mythic has been a term frequently used—popularity during the 1970s and 1980s was balanced with a backlash that began during the 1990s, where the international success of a younger generation of composers such as Kimmo Hakola, Jouni Kaipainen, Magnus Lindberg and Kaija Saariaho, whose complex music began to overtake Kokkonen's importance. For instance, while *The Last Temptations* continued to be staged, there was a marked decrease in the number of performances of his other works (although it should be noted that from 1990–95 Kokkonen's orchestral works were second only to Sibelius in number of performances by the ten major Finnish orchestras). Since 2000, however, there has been a discernable upswing in performances of his orchestral and chamber music, both within Finland and internationally.

While Kokkonen's importance to late twentieth-century Finnish culture as a political figure is beyond reproach, to what degree his music has been relevant to a succeeding generation of Finnish composers is more difficult to evaluate. For instance, while he was, for a period of time, associated with the Sibelius Academy and taught some of the most important post-1945 Finnish composers (possibly the only composition teacher who has taught more internationally known students is Paavo Heininen), none have directly imitated his distinctive harmonic palette or orchestral sound and, instead, have followed their own distinctive compositional trajectories. Further, Kokkonen's music, especially towards the end of his life, was criticized for its conservative musical surfaces—although the numerous analyses in this book demonstrate that this point of view clearly needs to be reexamined, for while the musical foreground of his works may not be as complex as the composers in vogue during the 1980s and 1990s, the underlying structure of this music can be extremely intricate. However, because he rarely spoke about the technical features of his music, this complex structure appears to have escaped the notice of virtually all commentators. In short, while Kokkonen's individual approach to harmony, form and orchestration may not have been imparted to the succeeding generations of Finnish composers—in other words, there is no "Kokkonen School" per se—his style has been without doubt prominent for a number of younger composers whose interest has been to create works that contain a narrative of symphonic argument reminiscent of models stemming back to such Viennese classicists as Beethoven, Haydn and Mozart (or from the twentieth century, Bartók, Shostakovich and, of course, Sibelius). Two of the most interesting and exciting are Kalevi Aho (b. 1949) and Mikko Heiniö (b. 1948).

The remarkable success of *The Last Temptations*, like Kokkonen's symphonies, may not have had a direct influence upon younger Finnish composers—works such as Kaija Saariaho's *L'amour de loin* or Kimmo Hakola's *The Mastersingers of Mars* are very far away from the sound, historical narrative, or overall compositional approach of Kokkonen's opera (both date from 2000). However, its initial success during the 1970s came at a particularly potent time in Finland's history (while we should recall that Aulis Sallinen also had a role to play in the birth of Finland's "opera boom," none of his operas match the extensive success of *The Last Temptations*), and the work's continued achievement in opera houses throughout Finland has played an important role in establishing a sympathetic environment in which younger Finnish composers are able to write operas without prejudice. As illustration, consider the floodgate of commissions for new opera productions that has continually grown in number since the 1970s.

In sum, Kokkonen's legacy rests as one of the most significant voices in twentieth-century Finnish music, whose challenging works such as *The Last Temptations*, the four symphonies, orchestral works such as *Music for String Orchestra*, *Sinfonia da camera*, *Opus Sonorum*, the cello concerto and *...durch einen Speigel...*, as well as such chamber works as the piano quintet and third string quartet occupy a vital position in Finland's remarkable lineage of twentieth-century composition. These pieces have had a strong performance history during his lifetime (in some cases, a spectacular record) and continue to appear in the opera house and concert hall. Further, Kokkonen's additional activities as a lecturer, teacher and administrator have made a profound mark upon his own, as well as the succeeding two generations of Finnish composers—no mean statement when one considers that Finland has produced one of the most vital bodies of orchestral literature by any country during the past fifty years.

Appendix

Chronological Listing of Works

Legend:
(GS)   G. Schirmer, Inc.
(WC)   Warner/Chappell Music Finland
(Ms)   manuscript

1936   Etude in Classical Style (piano solo) (Ms)

1938   *Pielavesi* (piano solo) (WC)

1938/40   Impromptu and Etude (piano solo) (Ms)

1940 (?) *Lulta ja minä* (voice/piano) (Ms)

1941   *Sans paroles* (voice/piano) (Ms)

1941/47   Three Little Songs from Poetry by Einari Vuorela (Ms) (voice/piano) (WC)

1943   Two Preludes (piano solo) (Ms)

1944   *Adagio* (voice/piano) (WC)

1944/53   Four Songs from Poetry by Uuno Kailas (voice/piano) (WC)

1948   *Häämarssi* (piano or organ solo) (WC)
           Piano Trio (violin/cello/piano) (WC)

1950   *Musiikkia Else Mattilan näytelmään "Autereentie 13-B"* (violin/piano) (Ms)

1951/53   Piano Quintet (2 violins/viola/cello/piano) (WC)

1953   Sonatina (piano solo) (WC)
           Ikivihreä (mixed choir) (Ms)

1955   *Duo* (violin/piano) (WC)
         Illat (voice/piano) (WC)

1956   *Religioso* (piano solo) (WC)
1956/57 *Music for String Orchestra* (WC)

1956/58/66 Four Children's Songs (voice/piano) WC)

1957   *Sonatella* (piano solo) (Ms)

1958   *Kotisisarten marssi* (female choir/piano) (Ms)

1958/59 *The Hades of the Birds* (mezzo-soprano/orchestra) (WC)
         String Quartet No. 1 (WC)

1958/60 Symphony No. 1 (WC)

1961   Symphony No. 2 (WC)

1961/62 *Sinfonia da camera* (twelve strings) (WC)

1963   *Sammakon virsi sateen aikana* (male chorus) (WC)
         Missa a cappella (mixed chorus) (WC)

1964   *Opus Sonorum* (orchestra) (WC)
         Lehvillä puiden (male chorus) (Ms)

1964/66 String Quartet No. 2 (WC)

1966   *Laudatio Domini* (mixed chorus) (WC)
         Kallein joululahja (voice/piano) (Ms)

1967   Symphony No. 3 (WC)

1968   Symphonic Sketches (orchestra) (WC)
         Hääsoitto (organ solo) (WC)
         Järvenpään kirkon kellosävelmä (ringing bells) (Ms)

1968/69 Five Bagatelles (piano solo) (WC)

1969	*Suruosoitto* (organ solo) (WC)
	Cello Concerto (WC)
	Amy (flute/trumpet/guitar/double bass/percussion/piano) (Ms)
	Erekhtheion (soprano/baritone/chorus/orchestra) (WC)
1970	Concertino (flute/strings/piano) (Ms)
1971	*Inauguratio* (orchestra) (WC)
	Symphony No. 4 (WC)
1972/73	*Sub rosa* (voice/piano) (WC)
1973	Woodwind Quintet (GS)
	Tontilo-kantaatti (children's voice) (Ms)
1973/75	*The Last Temptations* (WC)
1974	*Lux aeterna* (organ solo) (WC)
1975	Two Monologues from *The Last Temptations* (bass/orchestra) (WC)
1975/76	Cello Sonata (GS)
1976	String Quartet No. 3 (GS)
1976/77	*...durch einen Spiegel...* (harpsichord/12 strings) (GS)
1977	Four Interludes from *The Last Temptations* (orchestra) (WC)
1978	*Ukko-Paavon virsi* (wind ensemble arrangement of "Paavo's Hymn" from *The Last Temptations*) (WC)
1979	*Luxta crucem* (organ solo) (WC)
1979/81	Requiem (soprano/baritone/chorus/orchestra) (WC)
1980	*Ukko-Paavon virsi* (arrangement of "Paavo's Hymn" from *The Last Temptations* for baritone/children's choir/orchestra) (WC)
1982	*Improvvisazione* (violin/piano) (WC)

1984   Contrapunctus XI from *Art of Fugue* (arrangement for chamber orchestra) (Ms)

1984/85   *Sormin soitti Väinämöinen* (male chorus) (WC)

1986/87   *Il paesaggio* (chamber orchestra) (WC)

1991   Crescat in G (solo tuba) (Ms)

Bibliography

Aho, Kalevi, Pekka Jalkanen, Erkki Salmenhaara and Keijo Virtamo. 1996. *Finnish Music*. Helsinki: Otava.

Alho, Olli, ed. 1997. *Finland: A Cultural Encyclopedia*. Helsinki: Finnish Literature Society.

Drees, Stefan. 1999. "The Importance of Symphonic Processes: Primoridal Cells in the Early Works for Chamber Orchestra of Joonas Kokkonen." In *Topics, Texts, Tensions: Essays in Music Theory*. Edited by Tomi Mäkelä. Magdeburg: Otto-von-Guerichke-Universität.

Hako, Pekka. 1990. Liner notes for CD recording of *The Last Temptations*. Finlandia CD 104.

_____. 2001. *Voiko Varjo olla Kirkas: Joonas Kokkonen Elämä*. Helsinki: Ajatus Kirjat.

_____. 2002. *Finnish Opera*. Translated by Jaakko Mäntyjärvi. Helsinki: Finnish Music Information Centre.

Heiniö, Mikko. *Suomen musiikin historia 4: Aikamme Musiikki 1945–1993*. Helsinki: Werner Söderström.

Henell, Tero-Pekka. 1990. Liner notes for CD recording of *Symphonic Sketches*, Cello Concerto and Symphony no. 4. BIS CD-468.

_____. 1991. Liner notes for CD recording of *Music for String Orchestra, Hades of the Birds* and Symphony no. 1. BIS CD-485.

_____. 1991. Liner notes for CD recording of *Inauguratio*, Interludes from *The Last Temptations, Erekhtheion* and Symphony no. 2. BIS CD-498.

_____. 1991. Liner notes for CD recording of Requiem, *Opus Sonorum* and Symphony no. 3. BIS CD-508.

_____. 1991. Liner notes for CD recording of *...durch einen Spiegel...*, Woodwind Quintet, *Sinfonia da camera* and *Il paesaggio*. BIS CD-528.

_____. 1991. Liner notes for CD recording of String Quartets 1–3 and Piano Quintet. BIS CD-458.

Hepokoski, James. 1993. *Sibelius: Symphony no. 5*. Cambridge: Cambridge University Press.

Howell, Tim. 1989. *Jean Sibelius: Progressive Techniques in the Symphonies and Tone Poems*. New York: Garland.

Jackson, Timothy L. and Veijo Murtomäki. 2001. *Sibelius Studies*. Cambridge: Cambridge University Press.

Jurkowski, Edward. 1999. "The Symphonies of Joonas Kokkonen." *Tempo* 208: pp. 18–23.

_____. 2000. "Joonas Kokkonen's 'Free' Dodecaphonic Composition? A Study of the Passacaglia from the String Quartet no. 2." *STM-Online*. url: http://www.musik.uu.se/ssm/stmonline/vol_3/index.html

Karjalainen, Elina, ed. 1982. *Joonas Kokkonen—näköaloja luovuuteen ja ihmisyyteen.* Porvoo: WSOY.

Kokkonen, Joonas. 1988. "The Road to Mental Music." Translated by Susan Sinisalo. *Finnish Music Quarterly* 4/1988: pp. 38–41.

_____. 1992. *Ihminen ja Musiikki.* Edited by Kalevi Aho, Hanna Aho and Tero-Pekka Henell. Jyväskylä: Gaudeamus Oy.

Koponen, Glenn. 1980. "A Study of the Symphony in Finland from 1945 to 1975 with an Analysis of Representative Compositions." Ed.D. Dissertation, Columbia University Teachers College.

Korhonen, Kimmo. 1995. *Finnish Concertos.* Translated by Timothy Binham. Helsinki: Finnish Music Information Centre.

_____. 1995. *Finnish Orchestral Music 2.* Translated by Timothy Binham. Helsinki: Finnish Music Information Centre.

_____. 1995. *Finnish Composers since the 1960s.* Translated by Timothy Binham. Helsinki: Finnish Music Information Centre.

_____. 1997. *Finnish Piano Music.* Translated by Timothy Binham. Helsinki: Finnish Music Information Centre.

_____. 2001. *Finnish Chamber Music.* Translated by Timothy Binham. Helsinki: Finnish Music Information Centre.

Kuokkala, Pekka. 1992. *Ooppera Viimeiset kiusaukset Joonas Kokkonen säveltäjäkuvan heijastumana.* Jyväskylä: Jyväskylä yliopisto.

_____. 1998. Liner notes for CD recording of Piano Works. Alba Records, ABCD 127.

Marvin, Elizabeth West. 1988. "A Generalized Theory of Musical Contour: Its Application to Melodic and Rhythmic Analysis of Non-Tonal Music and its Perceptual and Pedagogical Implications." Ph.D. dissertation, University of Rochester.

Mead, William Richard. 1968. *Finland.* London: Ernest Benn Ltd.

Murto, Seppo. 1987. "Great Religious Works." Translated by Susan Simisalo. *Finnish Music Quarterly* 2/1987: pp. 22–24.

Murtomaki, Veijo. 1993. *Symphonic Unity: The Development of Formal Thinking in the Symphonies of Sibelius.* Helsinki: University of Helsinki.

Mäkelä, Tomi, ed. 1997. *Music and Nationalism in 20th-Century Great Britian and Finland.* Hamburg: von Bockel Verlag.

Mäkinen, Timo. 1986. "The Vital Importance of Technique." Translated by Susan Simisalo. *Finnish Music Quarterly* 4/1986: pp. 2–6.

Pokkinen, Ilmo. 1992. *"Orgaaninen Prosessi": Tutkimus Joonas Kokkosen motiivitekniikan ja muotoajattelun kehittymisestä.* Helsinki: Studia Musicologica Universitatis Helsingiensis IV.

Richards, Denby. 1968. *The Music of Finland.* Lontoo: Hugh Evelyn Ltd.

Salmenhaara, Erkki. 1997. "Finnish Music in the 20s and 30s: Internationalism vs. Nationalism." Article contained in Tomi Mäkelä, ed., *Music and Nationalism in 20th-Century Great Britain and Finland.* Hamburg: von Bockel Verlag.

Singleton, Fred. 1989. *A Short History of Finland.* Cambridge: Cambridge University Press.

Tyrväinen, Helena. 1993. "A l'ombre de Sibelius, Uuno Klami à Montmartre." *Boreales* 54–57: pp. 109–135.

_____. 2000. "Les origines de la réception de Debussy en Finlande (1901–1933)." *Cahiers Debussy* 24: pp. 3–23.

Solsten, Eric and Sandra Meditz. 1990. *Finland: A Country Study.* Washington DC: Library of Congress Publications.

Index of Works Discussed